Fodor's 90
Pocket
Guide to
Paris

Paul Ross
and
Simon Hewitt

GW00630852

FODOR'S TRAVEL PUBLICATIONS, INC.
New York & London

ISBN 0–679–01812–3

Fodor's Pocket Guide to Paris

Editor: Richard Moore
Drawings: Ted Burwell
Maps: Swanston Graphics
Cover Photograph: Owen Franken

Cover Design: Vignelli Associates

Special Sales

Fodor's Travel Publications are available at special discounts for
bulk purchases (100 copies or more) for sales promotions or
premiums. Special editions, including personalized covers,
excerpts of existing guides, and corporate imprints, can be created
in large quantities for special needs. For more information, write
to Special Marketing, Fodor's Travel Publications, 201 East 50th
Street, New York, NY 10022. Inquiries from the United
Kingdom should be sent to Fodor's Travel Publications, 30–32
Bedford Square, London WC1B 3SG.

MANUFACTURED IN THE UNITED STATES OF AMERICA
10 9 8 7 6 5 4 3 2 1

Pocket Guide
To Paris

Contents

Map of Paris

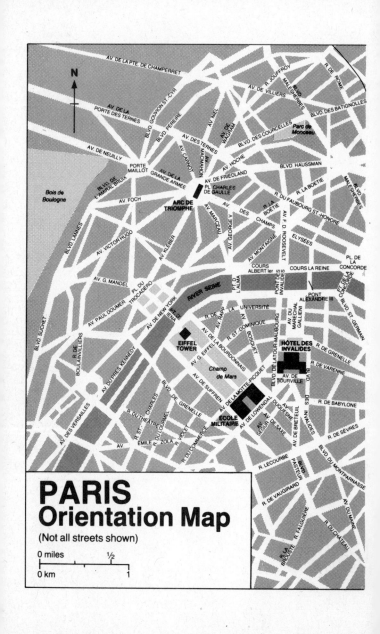

PARIS
Orientation Map

(Not all streets shown)

0 miles ½

0 km 1

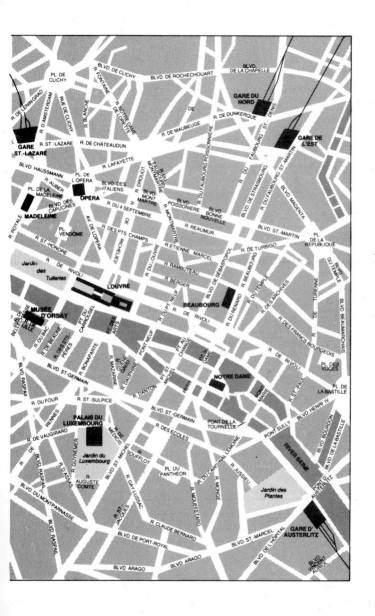

Paris Briefing

Make the French National Tourist Office the first stop on your visit to Paris. They can supply a wealth of information on the French capital, much of it free and all of it useful. Their principal offices are:

• **In the U.S.:** 610 Fifth Avenue, New York, NY 10020 (tel. 212–757–1125); 645 North Michigan Avenue, Chicago, IL 60611 (tel. 312–337–6301); 1 Hallidie, Suite 250, San Francisco, CA 94182 (tel. 415–986–4161); 9401 Wilshire Boulevard, Suite 314, Beverly Hills, CA 90212 (tel. 213–271–6665).

• **In Canada:** 1981 Avenue McGill College, Montreal, Quebec H3A 2W9 (tel. 514–288–4264); 1 Dundas Street West, Suite 2405, Box 8, Toronto, Ontario M5G 1Z3 (tel. 416–593–4717).

• **In the U.K.:** 178 Piccadilly, London W1V 0AL (tel. 01–491–7622).

You'll be equally well catered to in Paris itself. The main Paris Tourist Office is at 127 avenue des Champs Elysées, 75008 Paris (tel. 47-23-61-72). Open daily 9 A.M. to 8 P.M.; closed only at Christmas and on New Year's Day. The office is crammed with information on Paris and can also supply brochures for other parts of the country if you're traveling on. The multilingual hostesses can make hotel reservations in Paris for a small charge when you arrive, but they need eight days' notice to book you hotels outside Paris. In the same building you'll find the main office of the S.N.C.F. (French Rail) tourist office.

There is a special recorded-message telephone information service for details of the week's events—concerts, ballet, exhibits, parades, son-et-lumière, special events of all kinds. Called *Sélection Loisirs,* it offers a version in English, reached by dialing 47-20-88-98 (though you may need to listen to it twice round, as the pronunciation sometimes leaves a lot to be desired). The tourist office also publishes *Paris Selection,* a monthly review of cultural events, sightseeing in Paris, shopping, etc. *Saison de Paris* caters to the younger visitor, giving dates of pop concerts during the year. Both magazines are also available in some hotels and travel agencies.

There is also a tourist information office in the City Hall (just by Hôtel-de-Ville métro stop). And the City of Paris puts up posters all over the city giving details of one-time events— parades, firework displays, and the like. You name it, they organize it.

There are branch offices at Austerlitz, Est, Lyon, and Nord rail stations. Open Monday to Saturday year-round: 8 A.M.– 10 P.M. from Easter to end October; 8–8 the rest of the year. Gare du Nord is even open Sunday in summer from 1–8. An Eiffel Tower office is open Easter to September Monday to Saturday, 11–6.

• **What's On.** Information on what's on in Paris during your stay is best gleaned from the weekly *L'Officiel des Spectacles* or *Pariscope,* both available from all newsstands and drugstores, and full of information. Both appear on Wednesday, the day the movie programs change.

The national dailies *Le Figaro, Le Monde, Libération, La Croix,* and *France-Soir* give full details of movies, theaters, opera and ballet, exhibits, and other events. Other useful sources are the *International Herald Tribune,* published daily in Paris, and the English-language quarterly *Passion.*

Two booking services will find you a hotel anywhere in France: *Tradotel,* tel. 47-27-15-15, and *Resatel,* tel. 45-26-60-69. Resatel also offers tourist and business information, for example about museums, exhibitions, and trade fairs. Both services are free of charge.

MONEY MATTERS

Safeguard yourself by taking traveler's checks; be sure to note the serial numbers separately. But get some francs before you leave. The airport banks will be open whatever time you arrive, but there are usually long lines, and the rates aren't all that great anyway. Most Parisian banks are open from 9 to 4:30, Monday to Friday, though some close from 12 to 2. They often close on the day before a public holiday. Central Paris has a number of *bureaux de change,* many open late, but they will invariably give lower rates than a bank. Similarly, you can change money at hotels, some stores, and even the odd restaurant, but again you'll get a poor rate. You can also change money in some post offices (*bureaux de poste*) which are open 8 A.M.–7 P.M. weekdays and 8–12 on Saturday. Rates are similar to those given by the banks.

The major credit cards are accepted in most of the better hotels, restaurants and shops, but check the doors and windows for the usual stickers carefully. Visa, Diners Club, MasterCard, Eurocard, and Access are the most widely accepted, but some thrifty Parisian proprietors are damned if they see why they should pay over their hard-earned cash in a percentage to the credit card companies, and refuse to take *any* kind of card.

CLIMATE

Variable, as in most northern European countries. Summer can be hot, and most Parisians sensibly leave Paris to the tourists in August. Fall can be warm and mellow, and winter very cold with snow but also with beautifully clear, crisp days (on the other hand it can also be just plain awful). Spring brings contrasting spells of overcast skies with rain, and the clear blue skies which inspired the song *April in Paris.*

CLOTHES

The French are highly fashion conscious. Parisian chic is visible everywhere: in the street, restaurants, the opera, the métro. Choose clothes to fit the occasion, to feel comfortable whether you're going to a Gala night at the Opéra or spending the day sightseeing. But leave space in your case for anything you buy. And take an umbrella or raincoat and a pair of sunglasses.

TIME

France is six hours ahead of Eastern Standard Time and one hour ahead of Greenwich Mean Time. The French put their clocks forward an hour in the spring and back an hour in the fall at more or less the same time as both the U.S. and Britain.

ENTRY AND CUSTOMS

All foreign nationals must have a valid passport to enter France. American visitors no longer need to have a visa.

There are two levels of duty-free allowance for travelers entering France: one, for those coming from an E.E.C. country; two, for those coming from any other country.
• In the first category you may import duty free: (1) 300 cigarettes, 150 cigarillos, 75 cigars, 400 grams of tobacco; (2) three liters of fortified or sparkling wine, 5 liters of still table wine and one and a half liters of alcohol over 22° proof, or three liters of alcohol less than 22° proof; (3) 75 grams of perfume and three-eighths of a liter of toilet water; (4) for those over age 15, other goods to the value of 2,400 frs. (620 frs. for those under 15).
• In the second category you may import duty free: (1) 200 cigarettes, 100 cigarillos, 50 cigars, or 250 grams of tobacco (these allowances are doubled if you live outside Europe); (2) two liters of wine, and two liters of alcohol less than 22° proof, or one liter of alcohol more than 22° proof; (3) 50 grams of perfume and a quarter of a liter of toilet water; (4) for those over age 15, other goods to the value of 300 frs. (150 frs. for

those under 15). Any amount of French or foreign currency may be imported into and exported from France.

TIPPING

Hotels, restaurants, and cafés are now obliged by law to post net prices (*service compris, prix nets*), so you need no longer worry about the (15%) service charge. Tipping in a café usually entails leaving the waiter the small change brought back to you, if you think it's justified. In a restaurant, leaving a 5- or 10-franc piece (depending on the total bill) is considered a sign of appreciation for good service.

GETTING AROUND

• **From the Airports:** Getting into town from both the city's main airports—Roissy/Charles de Gaulle, the major airport, and Orly—is easy. There are buses from both every 12 minutes between 5.45 A.M. and 11 P.M. Buses from Roissy go to the Porte Maillot terminal in the northwest of the city, from Orly to Les Invalides terminal on the Left Bank. Journey times can vary from 30 to 90 minutes depending on the traffic.

There are fast R.E.R. trains to the Gare du Nord and central Paris from Roissy, and S.N.C.F. trains to the Gare d'Austerlitz and the St.-Michel from Orly. Trains leave every 15 minutes, and the trip takes about 30 minutes. All the airport trains link up with the R.E.R. express métro system, meaning that you can easily change onto the regular métro.

Taxis are plentiful at both airports and will take you into the center of Paris for around 180 frs., including tip.

• **City Transportation:** Modern Paris is a bustling, noisy city, full of traffic and very impatient drivers who hoot at everything that moves and who will park sideways up a wall if given a chance. You'll need the agility of a cat to avoid these two- and four-wheeled menaces. They are no respecters of pedestrians.

Having said which, the public transport system in Paris is excellent, *if* you can avoid the rush hours (8–9 and 4:30–6:30). The best way to get around is on the métro; it's fast, efficient, and clean. There are maps in every station, some of which will light up your route at the touch of a button. Look for the name of the station at the end of the line you take. For example, if you are traveling from the Gare du Nord to St.-Germain-des-Prés, you take the line marked "Direction Porte d'Orléans." At the time of writing there were eight *SITU* machines in or near main métro and R.E.R. stations. Punch in the name of the street, museum or site you want and a card will emerge telling you the best way to get there.

There are both first- and second-class cars, but, whichever you use, buy a *carnet,* a little book of ten tickets—29.60 frs. for second class, 45 frs. for first. They're less expensive than regular tickets and eliminate the need to wait in line. You can buy them at all stations, as well as on buses, and at tobacco counters (*tabac*). All tickets can be used on buses and the métro. With the exception of very lengthy bus rides, all trips are flat rate. Métro tickets are also good for the funicular railway up to Sacré-Coeur. Remember to keep your ticket with you after you've punched it into the automatic machine or you may be fined.

An excellent travel bargain is the Paris Visite pass, giving unlimited first-class travel on all métro and R.E.R. trains and buses. To travel in Paris and the inner suburbs costs 70 frs. for three days and 110 frs. for five days; to travel in the outer suburbs as well (including airports) costs 130 frs. and 160 frs. respectively. It is available from Roissy/Charles de Gaulle and Orly airports; the Paris tourist office; the head office of the R.A.T.P. (53 bis quai des Grands Augustins, 6e); and most métro stations. Alternatively, you can buy a weekly (*coupon jaune*) or monthly (*carte orange*) ticket, sold according to zone. Zones 1 and 2 cover the entire métro network (cost: 48 frs. a week; 167 frs. a month). For these tickets you need to get a pass (from rail and major métro stations) and provide two passport-sized photographs.

The bus network is good, even if journey times are longer than on the métro. But it's a good way of seeing the city, and as each bus has a map of its route inside, with every stop marked, you needn't worry about missing your stop. Ring the bell to ask the driver to stop if the red *Arrêt demandé* sign isn't already lit up.

Taxis are a problem in Paris, mainly because there aren't enough of them. You can hail them in the street if their lights are on, but the best plan is either to ask your hotel to call one for you, or to make for one of the city's numerous taxi ranks, easily identified by the blue-and-white TAXI sign. Very few cabs will take more than three passengers. Any cab without a meter should be viewed with suspicion. If you *do* take one, agree on the fare before you set off. If a taxi doesn't stop when you hail it, it's not because the driver dislikes tourists: he's probably on his way home and forgotten to turn his light off. By law French taxi drivers are not supposed to work more than 10 or 11 hours a day.

• **Excursions and Detours.** There are numerous city bus tours taking in all the main sights with commentaries in every language from Serbo-Croat to Eskimo. The place des Pyramides at the east end of the Tuileries is where most set off from. Best-known and most reliable companies are: *American Express,* 11 rue Scribe, 9e (tel. 42-66-09-99); *Cityrama,* 3 pl. des Pyramides, 1er (tel. 42-60-30-14); *Paris Vision,* 3 rue d'Alger, 1er (tel. 42-60-31-25).

For a more personal touch contact *International Limousines,* a luxury car or minibus service at 182 blvd. Péreire, 17e (tel. 45-74-77-12). They can take up to seven passengers round the city and the surrounding areas for a minimum of three hours at 200 frs. an hour. Reservations are essential.

Though sometimes crowded, a boat trip along the Seine is a marvelous way of seeing the city. There are a number of companies offering trips. Try: *Bateaux Mouches* (tel. 42-25-96-10), tours from the Pont de l'Alma, 8e, including evening trips with dinner (for which no children under 12 are allowed and "respectable" dress is encouraged); *Bateaux Parisiens-Tour Eiffel* (tel. 47-05-50-00), tours from the south end of the Pont d'Iéna, again including evening trips with dinner on Friday and Saturday: *Vedettes Paris Ile-de-France* (tel. 47-05-71-29/45-50-23-79), tours from the Port de Suffren; *Vedettes du Pont Neuf* (tel. 46-33-98-38), tours from the Square du Vert Galant in the middle of the Pont Neuf. In 1988 an experimental water-bus service, called *Bat-O-Bus,* was launched between the Eiffel Tower and the Hôtel de Ville. Unlike the *bateaux mouches,* this has several stops along the way. Price of tickets is a flat 30 frs.

Perhaps the ultimate tour around Paris is in a helicopter. *Hélicap* (tel. 45-57-75-51) have trips over Paris or La Défense on the western edge of the city or out to Versailles. Alternatively, they will devise a route of your choice, though

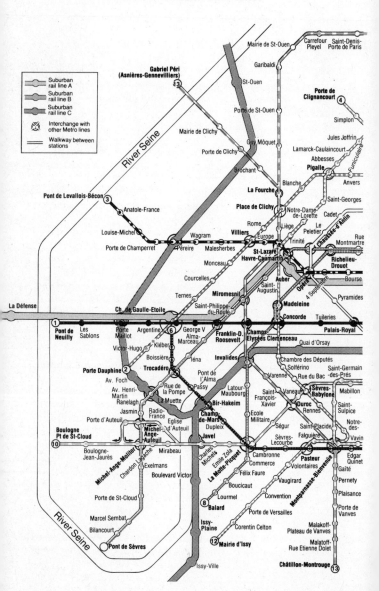

PARIS METRO

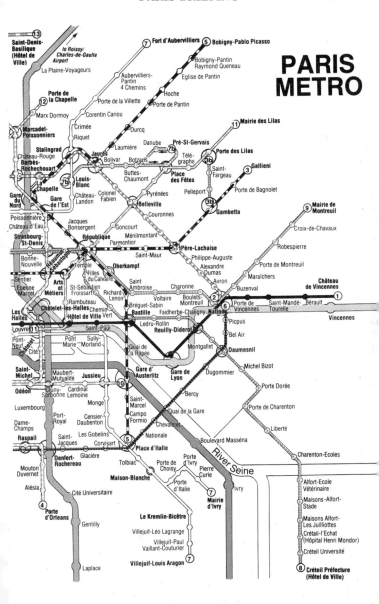

obviously the farther you go the more it costs. *Chainair* (tel. 39-56-20-11) offers a private jet service that will fly you wherever you like in France—for a price!

Back on terra firma again, bicycles can be rented from a number of places. Try: *La Maison du Vélo* (tel. 42-81-24-72); *Paris-Vélo* (tel. 43-37-59-22); and several main R.E.R. stations.

TAX REFUNDS

Visitors to France (i.e. those normally residing outside the country) may be given the opportunity to save money by being exonerated from part of the value-added tax (*T.V.A.* in French) on certain goods. Discounts obtained in this way range from 20%–30% (on "luxury" goods such as jewelry or perfumes). You should be aware that offering this discount is not a legal obligation of shopkeepers, so you may not insist on it. You'll find that the best places at which to benefit from the system are the department stores, which have special staff dealing with it, and shops with a large foreign clientele. Small boutiques are emphatically not equipped to deal efficiently with the complicated paperwork involved, and the system is liable to break down.

This is how it works. For a start, the total value of your purchases in a single store must be at least 1,200 frs. if you live outside the E.E.C.; if you live in an E.E.C. member state (which of course includes the U.K. and the Irish Republic), discounts are obtainable only on *single items* costing at least 2,400 frs. Some stores will simply state a price after deduction of the discount. But they'll be taking a risk, because if you don't do your bit by handing on the documentation to customs, they'll be out of pocket. The great majority will ask you to pay the full amount and the discount will be sent to you in due course. The store will fill out a form in quadruplicate, giving you three copies and keeping one. Make sure that if you live outside the E.E.C. the store hasn't filled in an E.E.C. form by mistake and vice versa. You must give details of your bank account, or that of friends in France—reimbursements cannot be made to private addresses. If you live outside the E.E.C. you present two of the forms to the customs official on leaving the country—he will probably ask you to see the goods in question to make sure that you haven't just been doing a favor to a French friend! Make sure to leave plenty of time for this operation. If you live in an E.E.C. country, the papers are dealt with by the customs official when you reach your own country.

Frankly, you may well think it's not worth the time and trouble, unless you're making really big purchases. And E.E.C. residents in particular should bear in mind that the customs official you present your forms to back home may decide to charge you customs duty on the goods—which will easily cancel out the V.A.T. refund!

Introducing Paris

Paris, according to Henry James, is "an immense, amazing spectacle . . . a very good place to spend a fortune . . . a very good place for idle people." Or, as Victor Hugo put it, "To err is human. To loaf is Parisian."

Paris is a city of wonderful contrasts, from the vast, gilded salons of Proust's world on the boulevard Haussmann and the avenue de Messine, to the narrow, tightly packed townhouses of the Left Bank, swamped in an air of venerable grandeur and faded pomp, where gardens lie between huge porches and high walls. There are the Grands Boulevards—and above all avenue Montaigne—where shop windows display opulent wares, stunning fashions, and jewelry; there are crammed bookshops in narrow streets winding down to the *bouquiniste* stalls along the Seine; there are tiny shops hidden to the left and right of the rue St.-Denis and the rue St.-Martin, stuffed with bric-à-brac, not 500 yards from the gaudy lights of peep-shows, strip-clubs, and the low life of the once splendid district of Les Halles, Zola's fabled "belly of Paris," today home to the huge, modern Forum shopping mall.

There are magnificent walks to take and unforgettable sights to see: the imposing setting and perfect symmetry of the obelisk in the place de la Concorde; the grandiose views through the Tuileries from the Louvre's glass pyramid, stretching away to the west and, continuing the architectural line, straight up the Champs Elysées to the Arc de Triomphe and the distant shadow of the colossal arch of La Tête Défense; the vast, soft-brown towers of Notre Dame, with its tortured gargoyles and magnificent portals leading to the splendid dimness inside; and in severe contrast, high on its hill, the startling whiteness of the Basilique du Sacré-Coeur. And then there is the brash Pompidou Center—Beaubourg—blatantly displaying its enameled, gaudy pipework and plastic tubeways above the narrow, medieval streets of the Marais.

All this—and more—is there for you to seek out. Or, if you are one of the "idle people," you can sit outside one of the thousands of boulevard cafés, and simply watch the world go by.

PARIS OVERVIEW

Paris is an accessible city, pleasant and easy to walk around. Most of the larger streets—the avenues or boulevards—lead to a satisfyingly designed *place,* or square. Many of the smaller streets run adjacent to, or parallel to, these, so that even if you make a wrong turn you eventually arrive at a recognizable landmark.

Snaking through the middle of the city, flowing from east to west, is the Seine, dividing Paris into the Right (or north) Bank and the Left (or south) Bank. The river has dominated the city's history from the time when the first settlers, the Parisii, made the Ile de la Cité, today the site of Notre Dame, their home in the 3rd century B.C. From then on trade centered around the river and its two islands (the Ile St.-Louis is the other, smaller island). It is apt that the symbol of Paris is a ship.

Gradually, through the years of Roman occupation and the Dark Ages, the city grew. Notre Dame, the Louvre, the University, the Sainte-Chapelle, the Marais, the Bastille, and

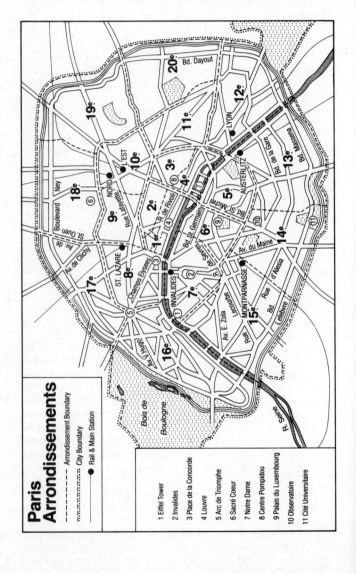

Paris Arrondissements

- – – – Arrondissement Boundary
- ·····-··-· City Boundary
- ●——— Rail & Main Station

1 Eiffel Tower
2 Invalides
3 Place de la Concorde
4 Louvre
5 Arc de Triomphe
6 Sacré Coeur
7 Notre Dame
8 Centre Pompidou
9 Palais du Luxembourg
10 Observatoire
11 Cité Universitaire

the Pont Neuf, all of them on or near the Seine, were among the earliest of the swelling city's districts and monuments.

By the time Louis XVI was deposed, in 1792, Paris had grown magnificent under the Bourbon kings. They had added the place des Vosges, the Luxembourg Palace and Gardens, the Palais Royal, and the Académie Française. Louis XIV, the Sun King, oversaw the building of Versailles, Les Invalides, the Salpêtrière Hospital, Gobelins, the Louvre colonnade, and the Comédie Française. His successor's, Louis XV's, reign gave to Paris the Panthéon, the Palais-Bourbon, and the place de la Concorde.

On July 14, 1789, the Bastille was stormed and the Revolution began. Louis XVI and Marie-Antoinette, his queen, were executed in 1793, and the Reign of Terror ensued, instituted by Robespierre, Danton and Marat. 2,800 "enemies of the Revolution" in Paris alone lost their heads, thanks to Dr. Guillotine's new machine. By 1794, however, Robespierre had been executed and in 1799 Napoleon was appointed First Consul. Under Napoleon, industry developed and the arts flourished. But the Corsican corporal, having spread the Revolution almost throughout Europe by virtue of his seemingly invincible Grand Armée, was himself defeated in 1815 at Waterloo, and the Bourbon monarchy restored.

Between 1815 and 1848 the Ourcq, St.-Denis, and St.-Martin canals were built and the first railway in France laid down, between Paris and St.-Germain-en-Laye. During the Second Empire, a further, even more wide-ranging, rebuilding program was put in hand, chiefly under the guiding hand of Baron Haussmann, but prompted by the ambitious, eccentric Napoleon III. Substantial areas were demolished as Haussmann drove his enormous and stately boulevards through the ancient city. The Opéra, Les Halles, Vincennes, and the Bois de Boulogne all took shape, as modern Paris emerged from the medieval city. It was now that the city was divided into its 20 *arrondissements,* or districts. 1855 saw the first Paris International Exhibition, followed by another in 1867, a showcase for the Second Empire.

Napoleon III bungled his way into oblivion in 1870, however, when a newly-unified and aggressive Germany invaded France and in 1871 captured Paris. But though the citizens were driven to eating rats—even the two elephants in the Botanic Gardens, Castor and Pollux, found their way onto Parisian menus—the city quickly recovered after the war and a new period of pomp followed. It culminated in the building of the Eiffel Tower—a "lonely suppository," as the writer Huysmans called it—and a great World Exhibition in 1889. The first line of the métro opened in 1900.

Paris escaped damage in World War I, but suffered much under the Nazi occupation 20 years later. Hitler's order to destroy the city, following the German retreat in 1944, was happily disobeyed by the German commander. The French— not least the Parisians—are justly proud of their Resistance fighters, many of whom carried on their secret war in the city's labyrinthine sewers, under the very feet of their conquerors.

PARIS MISCELLANY

Try to arrange your stay in Paris to coincide with the particular types of entertainment the city offers throughout the year. If, for example, you are keen on the theater, the opera, ballet, and art exhibits, there's not much point coming in August or the beginning of September. Practically the whole of Paris closes up shop then and heads off on vacation; even a good many restaurants are closed for two or three weeks during July and August. But if, on the other hand, you simply want to explore the city and its sights, August is an excellent time to visit, if sometimes very hot. The third week of September sees the start of the "artistic" season, with the pace heating up all the way through to Christmas. January and February, traditionally the dead months as far as tourism is concerned, can be an excellent time to visit, though it can be cold.

Though the center of the city will certainly occupy most of your time—this is where the greatest concentration of monuments, museums, and other places of interest are found—there are also a number of fascinating and famous places of interest a little farther afield, all of them easily reached from Paris. Versailles, Fontainebleau, Vaux-le-Vicomte, Malmaison, St.-Germain-en-Laye, Chartres, Reims, Giverny, and Rouen are all well worth visiting, either for a day or a little longer. The Paris tourist office can help with travel arrangements.

The Eiffel Tower and Champs Elysées

As you stand underneath this giant tower, symbol of Paris the world over, trying to decide whether or not to climb it, think of its height—320 meters, or 1,051 feet—its weight—7,000 tons—and the 52 tons of paint used every seven years to paint it. Think of the 1,652 steps to climb if the elevators aren't working or you don't feel like paying the 45 frs. to take the elevator to the third stage (you can pay 14 frs. to go to the first stage and 30 frs. to go to the second). Think of the view, too; up to 42 miles on a clear day (the best time, so they say, is as near as possible to sunset). Then think of the idiot, home-made wings strapped to his back, who plummeted to an early grave from the summit. Think of the fool who rode his bicycle down from the first stage, and of the mad mountaineer who scaled it. But then think that you'll be able to

17

go back home and tell your friends that you, too, went to the top of the Eiffel Tower. *Bonne chance!*

All three stages are open year-round from 10 A.M. to 11 P.M. There are elevators to all three stages (and stairs!), and long lines almost year round. There's an excellent restaurant on the second stage, the **Jules Verne,** separate entrance from the Pilier Sud (south corner)—see 7th Arrondissement in the Restaurant listings—shops on all the stages, and a bar at the very top for those who want to get higher still.

From the Eiffel Tower, cross the Pont d'Iéna to the **Palais de Chaillot.** The building looks like something from 1930s Russia. Drink in the way the Palais and adjoining Trocadéro are aligned symmetrically with the Eiffel Tower and the Champ de Mars across the river, with the weighty facade of the Ecole Militaire and, to the left, the great dome of Les Invalides, under which Napoleon lies buried. The broad terrace here is a marvelous place for taking photos of the tower and general river views. The Palais de Chaillot houses several museums: the **Musée de l'Homme,** the **Musée de la Marine,** the **Musée des Monuments Français,** and the **Musée du Cinéma,** where you will get a guided tour by the movie-mad curator.

Opening times for the museums in the Palais de Chaillot are: Musée de la Marine daily 10 to 6 except Tuesday and public holidays; Musée de l'Homme daily 9:45 to 5:15 except Tuesday, film shows every day at 3 except Tuesday and Sunday (but not in July and August); Musée des Monuments Français daily 9:45 to 12:30 and 2 to 5:15 except Tuesday; Musée du Cinéma daily except Monday for guided tours *only* at 10, 11, 2, 3, and 4.

If you're in the museum mood, walk along the avenue d'Iéna to the place d'Iéna, site of the **Musée Guimet.** The museum has some extraordinary Cambodian sculptures. But if Cambodian and Tantric Buddhist art leave you cold, try the **Musée d'Art Moderne** in the Palais de Tokyo opposite. Otherwise, walk right past the Guimet, carry on up the avenue d'Iéna to the Arc de Triomphe, and prepare yourself for another climb.

The Musée Guimet, 6 place d'Iéna, is open daily except Tuesday from 9:45 to 5:10. The Musée d'Art Moderne de la Ville de Paris, to give it its full name, in the Palais de Tokyo, is open 10 to 5:40 on Tuesday and Thursday through Sunday, and 10 to 8:30 Wednesday, and is closed Monday.

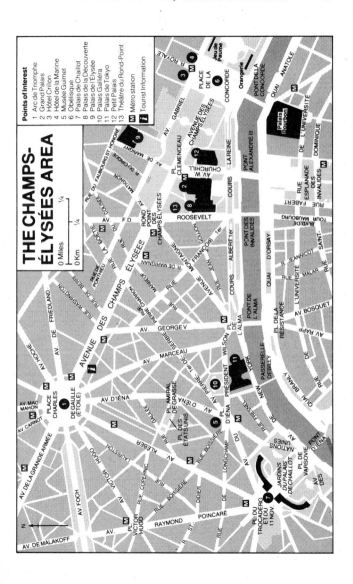

THE CHAMPS-ÉLYSÉES AREA

0 Miles   ¼
0 Km   ¼

Points of Interest

1 Arc de Triomphe
2 Grand Palais
3 Hôtel Crillon
4 Hôtel de la Marine
5 Musée Guimet
6 Obélisque
7 Palais de Chaillot
8 Palais de la Découverte
9 Palais de l'Élysée
10 Palais Galliéra
11 Palais de Tokyo
12 Petit Palais
13 Théâtre du Rond-Point

Ⓜ Métro station
ℹ Tourist Information

THE ARC DE TRIOMPHE

The original idea was to build a vast stone elephant with an amphitheater, banqueting hall, and apartments *inside* it. But, at Napoleon's command, this arch was built instead. When his new empress, Marie-Louise, was due to make her triumphal entry into Paris in 1810, the Arch was only a few feet above the ground. They were having trouble with the foundations. So, with typical Gallic aplomb, a vast, painted canvas replica of the Arch was hoisted up on a huge scaffold. Rumor had it that this same scaffold had been used at Marie-Antoinette's execution.

Take in the monumental relief sculptures covering the Arch, the names of all Napoleon's victories inscribed around them. At ground level is the **Tomb of the Unknown Soldier** with its eternal flame. A flyer called Godefroy flew his plane through the Arch in 1919. Inside, you can listen to and look at an audio-visual history of the Arch (French and English). And, if you've recovered from climbing the Eiffel Tower, climb the Arc de Triomphe. The view down the Champs Elysées and over Paris is well worth it.

The Arc de Triomphe is open daily 10 to 5 (6 in summer). There's a small extra charge for the audio-visual presentation and the elevator.

When you've done the Arch—and avoided those 12 death traps they call avenues, all of which converge here, by sensibly using the underpass—you are ready for the **Champs Elysées.** This incredibly wide avenue, offering one of the most spectacular views in Paris, is lined on both sides with banks, airline offices, cinemas, car showrooms, shopping arcades such as **Point Show** at 68 and **Les Champs** at 84, where you can eat, drink, shop, and watch a movie all at the same time. There are others: **Galerie du Lido, Galerie du Rond-Point, Galerie du Claridge** and **Galeries Elysées 26,** where you can buy exclusive fashions; definitely for the well heeled. A number of prostitutes—also well heeled—operate here, but they are so chic you could easily confuse them with high society Parisians.

As you amble toward the Rond-Point half-way down the Champs Elysées, you pass avenue George V on your right. Near the bottom of this street, on the left, is the **Crazy Horse**

Saloon. Further up, on the other side, is the attractive American church called the Holy Trinity, presenting you with a convenient choice between God and the Devil. The Crazy Horse is slick and slinky and lots of fun, though a bit expensive at 190 frs. for a drink at the bar, and 470 frs. for two drinks sitting down. They also charge an extra 15% for service. The Théâtre des Champs-Elysées, round the corner on avenue Montaigne, is much less expensive. It was built in 1913 and houses a main theater, specializing in opera and concerts, an auction-house and two other theaters: the Comédie des Champs Elysées, and the Studio des Champs Elysées. Entrance to this great complex is on avenue Montaigne.

Return to the Rond-Point on the Champs Elysées, towards the place de la Concorde. On your left is the **Marigny** and set back in the gardens on the south side is the **Rond-Point** theater, the new home of the famous Renaud-Barrault company. If you're not tempted by a play here, stop off for lunch. You'll enjoy soft music—jazz more often than not—and sophisticated salads.

Grab a snack if you're in the mood at **L'Hippopotamus,** 6 avenue Franklin-Roosevelt; it's cheap and cheerful, and has good steaks.

Opposite the Marigny is the **Grand Palais,** and, just down from that, the **Petit Palais,** two of the principal exhibit galleries in the city. Both are examples of the not-knowing-quite-where-to-stop school of architecture, especially the Grand Palais, a veritable Grande Dame of a building, overdressed with mosaics and an iron-and-glass roof.

The Grand Palais, avenue du Général-Eisenhower, is open Monday and Thursday–Sunday 10–8, Wednesday from 10 to 10, and closed Tuesday. The Petit Palais on the avenue Winston Churchill is open Tuesday–Sunday 10–5.40.

When you re-emerge, walk down the avenue Winston Churchill to the Pont Alexandre III, the broadest bridge in Paris as well as one of the most beautiful. Built for the Great Exhibition of 1900, the bridge has everything that characterized the Belle Époque: style, class, power, exuberance.

Back on the Champs Elysées, you approach the **place de la Concorde.** It opens out magnificently in front of the **Tuileries Gardens,** with the **Jeu de Paume** behind it to the left, and the **Orangerie** to the right, both continuing the architectural symmetry that began back at the Arc de Triomphe. This dramatic panorama of buildings, monuments, fountains, and sculptures gradually gathers momentum as it nears the place de la Concorde where it bursts forth in a symphony of grand and elegant architecture, the whole revolving around the one anachronistic feature in the design, the massive, 3,300-year-old obelisk of Luxor, placed exactly in the center of the place de la Concorde. And you should see it at night. The Parisians really do have a right to boast about their beautiful city.

The Tuileries
and the Louvre

From the place de la Concorde, the Tuileries Gardens stretch away to the east. In the distance you'll see the **Arc de Triomphe du Carrousel,** a scaled-down version of the Arc de Triomphe proper, at the west end of the Champs Elysées. Beyond it is the massive bulk of the Louvre whose arms enclose the new glass structure of the **Pyramide,** designed by the Chinese/American architect, I.M. Pei. Sit on one of those beautifully uncomfortable little metal chairs and soak it all in. It's one of the most amazing views in the whole city.

The **Jeu de Paume,** to the north, get its name from an early version of tennis that was popular in 17th and 18th-century France. It was long-famous as the Impressionist Museum, but, after extensive renovation and redecoration, it will be used to house temporary art exhibits. The fabled Impressionist collection (Manet, Monet, Degas, Gauguin, Renoir, Van

Gogh, Cézannne) has now been transferred to the new **Musée d'Orsay** on the other side of the river (see The Left Bank).

The **Orangerie,** the twin pavilion on the Seine side of the gardens, houses a fine collection of Impressionist and Modern art bequeathed to the French nation by a rich collector, as well as the superb **Water Lilies** series of paintings by Monet, the latter in a specially-built semicircular gallery.

After this visit you might enjoy an ice cream and/or a drink at the open-air café in the heart of the Tuileries.

LOUVRE BACKGROUND

Built in 1200 by Philippe Auguste, the **Louvre** was originally a fortress on the banks of the Seine. It was only in the 14th century that Charles V converted it into a private residence. He also added a magnificent library. François I, a compulsive builder, carried out more conversions from about 1527, and also laid out the gardens. In 1546 François then commissioned the architect Lescot to build him a completely new palace on the site of the Louvre, but the king died before the work could begin.

Over the next 300 years the building was variously remodeled, renovated, lived in, and neglected by a succession of French monarchs, among them Henri II, Catherine de Médicis, Henri IV, Louis XIII, and Louis XIV, whose idea it was to turn the place into a museum. Louis, of course, had moved his court out to Versailles. In his absence the Louvre was taken over by a colony of artists. Louis XIV expanded the palace to the east, building the beautiful **Colonnade du Louvre** and the perfectly-shaped **Cour Carrée,** the latter one of the most majestic parts of the whole complex.

The **Musée Central des Arts** was finally opened during the Convention in August 1794 at the end of the Revolution and quickly acquired a prestigious collection of masterpieces, dispersed in 1815 after Napoleon's defeat. During the Restoration (of the Monarchy) the collections were built up again and many of the sculptures in the **Musée des Monuments Français** were transferred here. Louis XVIII was the first of the restored kings, and the only French king to die in the Louvre. His successors didn't fare much better. Both Charles X and Louis-Philippe were expelled from the place by the French mob.

Napoleon III also added to the building. But in May 1871, during the bloody Paris Commune, insurgents set the place on fire, gutting the Marsan and Flore pavilions completely. Both were rebuilt under the Third Republic. This is how we see it today. Almost. A sci-fi transformation, a project called the "Grand Louvre," was started in 1983 and is due for completion in 1992. The main aims are to equip the museum with an infrastructure capable of catering to millions of tourists; to improve the presentation of the collections—hundreds of works of art have been gathering dust in the basement for years; and to redesign the Tuileries Terrasses. The main entrance to the galleries, Pei's glass pyramid, was completed in 1989; the underground galleries (Nord-Sud Carrousel-Tuileries) and a vast car park should be finished by the end of 1991.

LOOKING AROUND THE LOUVRE

The Louvre's catalog lists 300,000 items, give or take a few. If you manage to see 300 properly you will have done well, and can feel as proud as you did when you climbed to the top of the Eiffel Tower.

The **Grand Gallery** is on the second floor. It is the longest gallery in the world. It's 300 meters long, nearly 1,000 feet from the **Apollo Gallery** to the **Pavillon de Flore.** Begin at the Apollo Gallery. Look at the paintings first. You enter through the **Salles** (or "rooms") **Percier & Fontaine,** having passed the statue of *The Winged Victory of Samothrace* (best-known as the inspiration for the little figure above the grille of every Rolls-Royce). You are now entering the realms of French 14th-century painting: the *Portrait of Jean le Bon* (1360) against a gold background is the first realistic portrait of a French king. On to the **Salon Carré,** where you will find the 15th-century *Avignon-Pietà,* a poignant and beautiful masterpiece. In the next small room, looking out over the Seine, are French 16th-century paintings. Then you arrive at the **Grand Gallery,** where you see works by La Tour, Poussin, Claude Lorraine, Le Brun, and other 17th-century French masters. Turn right into the **Salle des États** for the Italian 16th-century and the *Mona Lisa.* You'll have to fight your way through crowds of supplicants to get a glimpse of her

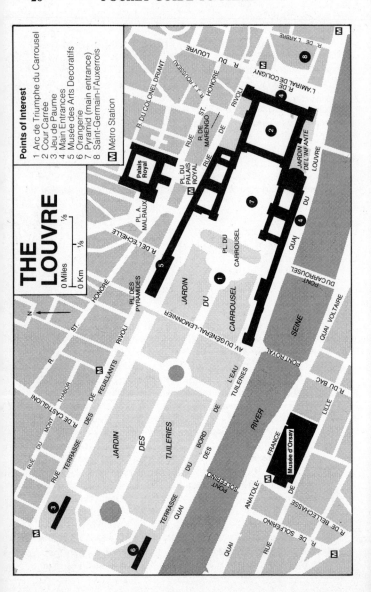

THE LOUVRE

Points of Interest

1 Arc de Triumphe du Carrousel
2 Cour Carrée
3 Jeu de Paume
4 Main Entrances
5 Musée des Arts Decoratifs
6 Orangerie
7 Pyramid (main entrance)
8 Saint-Germain-l'Auxerrois
Ⓜ Métro Station

0 Miles   ⅛   ¼
0 Km

behind her reflective glass; better to concentrate on the Titians.

Pass behind the screen at the end, behind Veronese's enormous *Wedding at Cana,* into the **Salle Denon,** and then turn right into the **Salle Daru,** where you will be confronted by Géricault's dramatic *Raft of the Medusa* and Delacroix's *Massacres of Chios.* Go back through the Salle Denon and into the **Salle Mollien** for more French neo-Classicism: David's great polemics and Ingres's ravishing nudes.

Continue through the **Mollien Wing** and have a quick look at the paintings by Greuze before you rejoin the Grand Gallery. On your left are a number of Watteau's and Fragonard's delectable 18th-century scenes of courtly dalliance. On your right is one of the most splendid collections of Italian paintings assembled in one gallery: Giotto, Fra Angelico, Botticelli, Bellini, Guardi. In the midst of these you will find Flemish, Dutch, and German paintings from the 15th to 17th centuries. Be sure not to miss Rubens' heroic series illustrating the life of Catherine de Médicis. Its scale and imaginative power are breathtaking.

From now on you are on your own. The first floor houses Greek and Roman antiquities—including the *Venus de Milo*—as well as Egyptian and Oriental works. More Greek and Roman antiquities can be found on the second floor, grouped around the Cour Carrée, as are the French Crown Jewels in the Apollo Gallery. Up on the third floor you'll find temporary exhibits and graphic art, and some more French and English 17th- to 19th-century paintings. Finally, on the first floor of the **Pavillon des Etats** and the **Pavillon de Flore,** there are substantial collections of French sculpture, dating from the early medieval period to the 19th century, and foreign sculptures, among them pieces by Cellini and Michelangelo.

The Louvre is open every day, 9–6 (9–9:45 Mon. and Wed.), except Tuesday and public holidays. There's an entry fee of 25 fr.; Sunday is free. There are guided tours every day except Sunday at 10:30 and 3 from the Information Desk at the main entrance; 20–25 frs. Nearest métro is Palais Royal.

Having successfully conquered the Louvre, you may like to head for an eating place! Try the rue St.-Honoré or around the place du Marché St.-Honoré. Both are filled with good restaurants offering a wide spectrum of specialties and prices.

Around the Opéra

This stage in our exploration of Paris begins at the **Palais Royal,** located immediately to the north of the Louvre. The Palais was built by Richelieu in the 17th century as his Paris residence—its size and sumptuousness give a potent idea of the power and wealth grabbed by the wily Cardinal. It subsequently passed into the hands of the regent Philippe, duke of Orléans, in whose tender care it became the scene of crazed revels and orgies. Thereafter it was owned by Philippe Egalité, duke of Orléans. Needing to raise money, he built a series of delightful town houses around the garden with first-floor arcades. These were intended as shops for the honest artisans of the city but quickly became the haunts of gamblers and prostitutes. Today, with the Palais Royal itself occupied by various government departments, Buren's stumpy, candy-striped columns add the only wayward note.

Despite their central location, the rose-filled gardens are an island of calmness and serenity, their elegant arcades providing welcome shade on a hot day. There's a pretty little

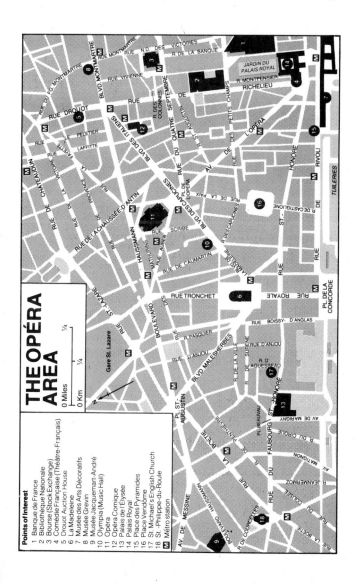

Points of Interest

1 Banque de France
2 Bibliothèque Nationale
3 Bourse (Stock Exchange)
4 Comédie Française (Théâtre-Français)
5 Drouot Auction House
6 La Madeleine
7 Musée des Arts Décoratifs
8 Musée Grevin
9 Musée Jacquemart-André
10 Olympia (Music Hall)
11 Opéra
12 Opéra Comique
13 Palais de l'Elysée
14 Palais Royal
15 Place des Pyramides
16 Place Vendôme
17 St Michael's English Church
18 St.-Philippe-du-Roule
Ⓜ Métro station

fountain in the center of the garden and sandpits at the north end for children. You'll also find those ubiquitous little metal chairs, beloved by the French municipal authorities. The **Montpensier Gallery** along the west side of the gardens contains several cafés and restaurants.

The first courtyard, if you enter from the south, is one of the talking points of Paris. It was transformed in 1986 into a huge piece of sculpture, designed by Daniel Buren. A small forest of black-and-white-striped stone pillars, checkerboard paving, and hidden lights and water, challenge the pompous pillars that surround the court with a series of perspective tricks. Like so many public displays of modernism in Paris, it's startling and done with great style. It also cost the earth to accomplish!

Leave the gardens at the north end and venture into the quaint and cobbled rue de Beaujolais, site of **Le Grand Véfour,** a gastronomic experience on the grand scale. For full details, see First Arrondissement in the Restaurant listings.

You can make an intriguing detour here to the **Comédie Française.** Turn left down the rue de Montpensier, head past the little Théâtre du Palais Royal on the corner, and walk down the side of the Palais Royal to the place André-Malraux and the Comédie Française. The Comédie Française is the lone hub of traditional French comedy. The company doesn't restrict itself to comedy, however, and its repertoire also includes the likes of Racine and Corneille—in other words, all the heavyweights of French drama—plus a fair sprinkling of modern works both French and foreign. But, as befits an organization founded by Louis XIV—in 1680 to be exact, though it moved here only at the end of the 18th century—whose primary purpose was to spread far and wide the glories of the French stage, productions are still decidedly mannered and stagey. And of course in French.

Back on the rue de Beaujolais, head north up the little **passage des Deux Pavillons.** It's not much more than a flight of steps, and hardly altered over the centuries. This brings you onto the rue des Petits Champs. (Try the **Bistrot Vivienne** here—an excellent place for a snack.) Heading right down the rue des Petits Champs you arrive at the **place des Victoires,** one of the most beautiful of Parisian squares.

There's an early 19th-century equestrian statue of the Sun-King in the center of the square, gazing at a clutch of expensive clothes shops, among them Kenzo, Thierry Mugler and

Victoires. Make your way back down the rue des Petits Champs and into the **Galeries Vivienne** and **Colbert.** They're a pair of covered shopping malls containing a miscellaneous array of antique and collectors' shops: books, coins, maps, medals, pipes, etc., which make an intriguing diversion. Nearby is the modern and charming **A Priori-Thé,** a tea-shop typical of the new vogue that's sweeping Paris.

Next to the Galérie Colbert is the **Bibliothèque Nationale,** the National Library. It houses one of the world's greatest collections of historical prints, manuscripts, engravings, photographs, medals, cameos, bronzes, coins, records, tapes, and talking machines, as well as about nine million books, the earliest dating from the 15th century, including a copy of every French book published since 1537. Here you will find two Gutenburg Bibles, first editions of Pascal, Villon, Rabelais, Charlemagne's Gospel, and original manuscripts by the likes of Marie Curie, Victor Hugo, and Pasteur, to name but a few. Both the building and its contents are a veritable feast for the eyes. Take a look through the glass into the magnificent Second Empire Reading Room, with its cathedral-like domed ceiling and cast-iron columns.

The Bibliothèque Nationale entrance in the rue de Richelieu is open every day except public holidays from 9 to 4:30. The same entrance is used for exhibits. The entrance to the photography gallery is at 2 rue Vivienne or 6 rue des Petits-Champs, 2e. The **Musée Charles Cros,** a gramophone museum, opened in the fall of 1988.

Out of the Bibliothèque, continue north up the rue de Richelieu, crossing the rue St.-Augustin and the rue du Quatre Septembre, and turn right down the small, elegant rue des Colonnes. Here, at the end and to the left, you will find the public entrance to the **Bourse,** the Paris Stock Exchange. Don't be fooled by the classical serenity of the building. It's a madhouse inside. Head up to the public gallery from where the pandemonium on the floor is spread out below you: lunatics, all impeccably dressed, gesticulating wildly and shouting "J'ai!" or "Je prends!" at the top of their voices, speed around and jump up and down. These characters are the Wall Street wizards of Paris.

The Bourse is open Monday to Friday (guided tours every half hour, 11–1)—take your passport.

Not surprisingly, expense account lunching is the order of the day around the Bourse, and the area is packed with excellent, if expensive, restaurants. Try one and you may find yourself sitting next to one of the aforementioned maniacs. See Second Arrondissement in the Restaurant listings for full details.

For a very different type of eating experience walk up to the rue Feydeau, immediately north of the Bourse. Here, at #5 opposite the entrance to the passage des Panoramas, is a tiny old restaurant, apparently nameless. All that distinguishes it are the words "Restaurant Vins." You'd easily think you were walking into a private home as you push the door open. The food, like the atmosphere, is deeply traditional. The passage des Panoramas is itself full of small restaurants, ranging from inexpensive self-service joints, to the **Trattoria Toscana** for traditional Italian food.

Leave the passage des Panoramas and head into the busy boulevard Montmartre. Directly opposite is the **Musée Grévin,** the wax-works museum, so-called because it was founded by the caricaturist Grévin in 1882. This is a wonderfully tacky place to come to grips with Parisian history, with 20 kitsch scenes highlighting the building of the Eiffel Tower, the nightclubs of Montmartre, and a variety of exotic environments, each more ludicrous than the last. A grotto, complete with distorting mirrors, provides the *pièce de résistance.*

The Musée Grévin is at 10 boulevard Montmartre and is open daily 10–7.

As you walk west down the boulevard Montmartre, make a quick detour down rue Drouot to the Paris auction-house, the **Hôtel Drouot.** A dozen auctions—catering for all tastes and purposes—are held here daily. Then walk back to the boulevard and head left along the boulevard des Italiens, passing the Salle Favart on your left, the second home of the Paris Opéra.

Continue down boulevard des Italiens and you arrive at the place de l'Opéra, where the **Palais Garnier,** the Paris Opéra house, is resplendent in all her overblown finery. The Paris Opéra has been resident in this magnificent building since 1872, when Charles Garnier completed his grand Napoleon III-style palace. Beneath the cellars is a submerged lake, den of the Phantom of the Opéra. Above, the facade is a riot of columns, friezes, winged figures, busts, and sundry ornaments. Inside, the building is all marble, huge staircases, chandeliers, gilt decorations, caryatids holding up elaborate candelabra, tiers of arches, and galleries—don't miss Chagall's painted auditorium ceiling; then there is the room with parquet and mirrors, where spectators (of the Opéra and of each other) parade themselves in their Sunday best. On the subject of which, there's no point even trying to get into the Opéra for a First Night, a Gala, or a Subscription performance in anything less than a tux—"un smoking" as the French have it—or your best tiara. Open daily 11–4:30.

THE MADELEINE AND
PLACE VENDOME

From the place de l'Opéra head down the boulevard des Capucines, which in turn becomes the boulevard de la Madeleine, to the place de la Madeleine and **La Madeleine** itself, or to give it its proper name, the Church of St. Mary Magdalene. It looks like a Greek temple but could just as easily have looked like a great many other things if the people connected with its early history had had their way. Two buildings were begun here—the first modeled on the Invalides, the second on the Panthéon—but both were razed to the ground when not much more than the foundations had been laid. Then, in 1837, when the present building was nearing completion, it almost became Paris's first railroad station. Happily it escaped this ignominious end, and in 1842 was finally consecrated. Fate had one further twist in store, however: in 1871 the rioting mobs of the Commune shot and killed the priest.

Walk all round the outside. It's a magnificent sight, with 52 giant Corinthian columns, each 66 feet high, supporting a powerfully sculptured frieze. From the top of the monumental flight of steps that leads to the main entrance there's a satisfying view down the rue Royale to the place de la Concorde and on to the Palais Bourbon and the dome of the Invalides on the other side of the Seine. The huge, bronze doors are equally magnificent, with reliefs of the Ten Commandments. The interior is dim and somber, with the single nave crowned by three shallow domes. There is a flower market next to the church, and two food halls of fame, **Fauchon** and **Hédiard,** selling posh nosh and specialty products from France and exotic goodies from other parts of the world.

Crossing the rue Royale, just south of the place de la Madeleine, is the **rue du Faubourg St.-Honoré.** This is one of the most famous shopping streets in Paris, with St.-Laurent, Hermès, Lanvin, and Helena Rubinstein rubbing shoulders with art galleries (also on avenue Matignon) and antique shops. The fashion houses are situated mainly around the rue Royale and the rue de l'Elysée.

Going east along Fbg. St.-Honoré you arrive at the **place Vendôme.** Originally there was a statue of Louis XIV in the center of the square. This was destroyed in the Revolution and replaced by the bronze column, modeled on Trajan's Column in Rome, commemorating Napoleon's victories in Germany. This, too, was pulled down during the Commune, then put back up again. Napoleon's statue is on the top, looking out at the jeering faces carved on the keystones over the arches around the square.

The place Vendôme was designed for Louis XIV by Jules Hardouin-Mansard. All the facades of the square are uniform, with arcades at ground level, Corinthian pilasters rising through two storys, and roofs with dormer windows. Chopin died at #12. Today, the square is filled with expensive shops, including great jewelers like Boucheron and Van Cleef & Arpel, art dealers, the Ministry of Justice, and the Ritz Hotel. They combine to create an almost palpable air of power, wealth, and beauty. It's very Parisian and very desirable.

THE GRANDS BOULEVARDS

The rue de la Paix heads northeast out of the place Vendôme. It takes you back to the place de l'Opéra and the Grands Boulevards: Capucines, Italiens, Montmartre, Poissonnière, Bonne-Nouvelle, St.-Denis, and St.-Martin. The more easterly boulevards are now a bit down at heel and tawdry, so serious shoppers should head for the areas just north and southwest of the Opéra. Directly north of the Opéra is the **boulevard Haussmann,** an enormous thoroughfare where the traffic never seems to give way, stop or slow down. Haussmann was the man who razed half of Paris to the ground between 1852 and 1870. His great redevelopment scheme was by no means all bad. Paris may have lost some of its old quarters and fine buildings, but it gained Les Halles, all its principal railroad stations, the Bois de Boulogne and Vincennes, the Opéra, the sewers, the completion of the Louvre, its 20 arrondissements and, of course, its boulevards. One last word about Haussmann: when you walk down rue du Faubourg

St.-Honoré take a look at the 12 steps that go *up* to the entrance of the church of St.-Roch. Before Big Baron Haussmann battered his way through, the entrance to this church was *down* seven steps.

There's a cluster of department stores round the back of the Opéra waiting for anyone who's managed to cross the boulevard Haussmann: Galeries Lafayette, Marks and Spencer, and Au Printemps (the top-floor restaurant here has *artnouveau* decor and a wonderful stained-glass cupola).

South of the Opéra, down the **avenue de l'Opéra,** you'll find a further collection of elegant shops—jewelers and perfumers—and several good terrace cafés. At the end of the avenue de l'Opéra is the Palais Royal and the Comédie Française—more or less where you started out.

From here the **rue de Rivoli** runs eastwards towards the Châtelet and the Hôtel de Ville, and westwards back towards the Tuileries and the place de la Concorde. Again, shopping is the major attraction here. Walk the length of the rue de Rivoli under the beautiful arcades past all types of luxury and souvenir shops. Both **W.H. Smith** and **Galignani** have an excellent range of English books.

Montmartre

To reach Montmartre, take the métro to Anvers, head north up the little rue Steinkerque, and turn left at the place St.-Pierre. From here there are four routes. If you're feeling energetic, take the rue Foyatier and climb up the "Butte," the mound, to **Sacré-Coeur.** It's a beautiful climb but—be warned—very tiring. Alternatively, you can walk up through the gardens that lead directly to Sacré-Coeur. This is still quite a climb, but a good deal less exhausting. You can also take the rue Ronsard and the rue Paul Albert up on the east side of Montmartre. It's an attractive walk, with tiny cafés along the way. Finally, there's the easiest route of all. Take the funicular!

The name Montmartre is believed to be a corruption of *mont des martyres,* the martyrs' mount, a reference to the beheading here of St.-Denis in AD 272. (The story runs that St.-Denis subsequently marched, severed head in hand, to what is now the less than lovely district of St.-Denis about four miles north of Montmartre.) The name may equally well refer to a Roman temple to Mercury that is believed to have been here.

Be that as it may, Montmartre has always been a place apart from the rest of Paris, a fact that may well be one of the main reasons for its popularity among artists in the 19th and early 20th centuries. Before that, however, Montmartre—or the Butte, as the locals have it—was famous mainly for a Benedictine convent, founded in the 12th century. Henry IV, then king of Navarre, used it as his base when he tried to seize Paris in 1589. (As it turned out, his only conquest was the 17-year-old abbess.) In 1794, the convent was destroyed by the godless mobs of the Revolution, the last abbess was guillotined, and the name of the hill was changed to Mont-Marat, in honor of the man in the bath tub.

Today, of course, Montmartre is famous for three things. First, the basilica of Sacré-Coeur, built at the end of the Franco-Prussian war in 1870 as a symbol of national revival, and either hideous or beautiful (opinions have long been violently divided). Second, as an artistic quarter, full of painters and saucy Frenchmen in cafés. (In fact, though Montmartre once genuinely was the haunt of poets and painters, and the scene of bacchanalian revels that scandalized the bourgeoisie, these days any artistic activity is conducted on a strictly commercial basis for the exclusive benefit of the tourists who flock here in the vain hope of finding someone—anyone—who answers, however distantly, to the description of an artist.) Third, of course, there's the nightlife, covering the entire spectrum from the positively institutionalized respectability of the Moulin Rouge to the lowest of low lifers, lurking in doorways and dingy clubs.

At the top of the rue Foyatier steps make a right and you arrive at the Parvis du Sacré-Coeur. A short climb brings you to the gleaming white basilica. If you climb into the dome, there is a really magnificent view over Paris as well as a bird's eye view of the interior of the church.

Walk around the back of the church to the north side of the hill, and you enter a series of more peaceful streets leading down the northern flank of the hill and round to the **place du Tertre.** A host of artists will accost you here and offer to paint your portrait or your caricature. Those who have their easels firmly planted on the square proper theoretically have a license to do so and regular checks usually prevent them from asking extortionate prices, but be wary of others. If you do succumb, shop around and agree on a price *first.*

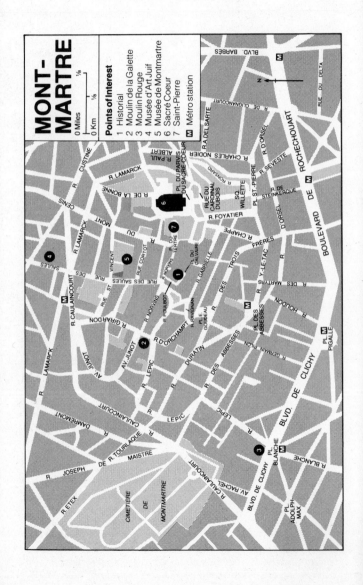

MONT-MARTRE

0 Miles ⅛ ⅙
0 Km ⅙ ⅛

Points of Interest
1 Historial
2 Moulin de la Galette
3 Moulin Rouge
4 Musée d'Art Juif
5 Musée de Montmartre
6 Sacré Coeur
7 Saint-Pierre
M Métro station

The square is lined with cafés and restaurants, fast-food and sandwich bars. **La Mère Catherine** and **La Crémaillère** are tourist-oriented but better than most, and **Chez Ma Cousine** and **Chez Plumeau** round the corner on the pretty place du Calvaire have first-rate cabarets.

Just down the northern side of the hill on rue Cortot is the **Musée du Vieux Montmartre.** The building was originally home to many artists. Today it is full of mementos from the district. It's open daily except Monday 2:30–6, and Sunday 11–6. Its back windows overlook the only remaining vineyard in Paris and the **Lapin Agile,** a little café that was long one of *the* artists' rendezvous in Paris. Though inevitably commercialized, it has survived surprisingly well. In fact, this little corner of Montmartre still exudes a village atmosphere quite unlike anywhere else in the city.

The **St. Vincent cemetery** is nearby on rue des Saules, but is tiny compared to the *Cimitière de Montmartre* farther along the rue Caulaincourt. Here you can visit the tombs of many of the famous people associated with Montmartre: Zola, Berlioz, Dumas (son), Degas, Offenbach, Stendhal, Alphonsine Plessis (better known as The Lady of the Camelias or "La Traviata"), and French film director François Truffaut.

The boulevard de Clichy, south of the twisty streets of Montmartre proper, is a lively center of nightlife. But here even the vaguest attempt to be Parisian, artsy or "Bohemian" has been abandoned. This is Times Square dumped straight into Paris. That's not to say you'll find only clip joints, amusement arcades, and painted ladies among the neon and the glitter, but it's no place to linger with a full wallet. The **Moulin Rouge** is here on the place Blanche, and the **Folies Bergère** is directly south on the rue Richer about half a mile away. Both are still going strong and presenting ever more lavish shows à la Vegas for the benefit of tourists from all over the globe (the Moulin Rouge recently, until the animal welfare people stepped in, had a dolphin leaping from a tank to pluck the clothes from a girl perched above it). But La Belle Époque it is not.

However, this corner of the world does boast one little cultural highlight, the **Musée Gustave Moreau.** This is in the rue de la Rochefoucauld, south of the place Pigalle. Moreau, leading light of the Symbolist movement, lived here for 46 years until his death in 1898. Anyone interested in the wilder flights of late 19th-century Romanticism should take a look. The museum is open daily except Tuesday and 1 Nov., 10–12:45 and 2–5:15.

If you feel like a complete change, take the métro to Jaurès, a mile or more to the east, and walk down the avenue Secrétan to the **Parc des Buttes-Chaumont.** Here you can relax in the surprisingly romantic park, laid out—by Haussmann—on the site of a disused quarry. Steeply-sloping woods, a lake with a rocky island, numerous walks, and a good restaurant—the **Pavillon du Lac**—complete the picture.

On the other side of the Jaurès métro stop is the **St.-Martin canal,** built to link the Seine with the Ourcq canal. It is still a working canal, and the stretch between Frédéric Lemaître square and the rue Bichat transports the onlooker into Amsterdam. It is serene, leafy, and picturesque, with hump-backed bridges. Boat trips along the canal are organized by Quiztour, 19 rue d'Athènes 9e (tel. 48-74-75-30).

Finally, for another detour, head down to the **Musée Edith Piaf** at 5 rue Crespin-du-Gast in the 11th arrondissement (nearest métro is Ménilmontant). Memorabilia, clothes, and photos have all been lovingly assembled by fans of "La Môme de Pigalle" to form a moving display. Visits by appointment only Monday to Thursday: tel. 43-55-52-72.

Beaubourg and the Marais

The walk around this neighborhood begins with the Forum
Shopping Complex and Beaubourg, two of the most modern
buildings in the city. It then covers the Marais, most elegant
of the city's aristocratic quarters. It is a walk in which history
and modernity lie cheek by jowl.

THE FORUM AND BEAUBOURG

Running north between the Forum to the west and Beaubourg, or the **Centre National d'Art et de Culture Georges
Pompidou** to give its full name, to the east is the boulevard
de Sébastopol.

The **Forum,** opened in the early '80s, stands on the site of Les Halles, Baltard's great 19th-century food market. Built largely below ground level, it's packed with excellent shops, cafés, and restaurants. You'll either love or hate the architecture—a mishmash of modern styles that don't always marry with harmony. The cascading effect of the three floors of the Forum itself are attractive and photogenic. In 1987 a whole new complex (Nouveau Forum) opened. Sober and sophisticated—even the information signs are elegantly designed—it boasts new boutiques, a tropical garden, an auditorium, and an Olympic-sized swimming-pool.

For a glimpse of history before you come to grips with more ultra-modernity, walk up the boulevard de Sébastopol a couple of blocks and turn right into the rue du Bourg l'Abbé, which in turn becomes the rue Montmorency. Here, on your right at #41, is the house of alchemist **Nicholas Flamel.** Built in 1407 as a charitable institution, it's reputed to be the second-oldest house in the city (the oldest is just round the corner in the rue Volta, but it's very much less interesting to look at and is, in any case, a private residence).

Continue down the rue Montmorency, turn right into the rue Beaubourg, and head down to the Pompidou Center itself. By now you are surrounded by acrobats, fire-eaters, fakirs, singers, clowns, break-dancers, performing dogs, budgerigars, monkeys, hippies, beatniks, punks, groupies, debs, androids, and tourists. The occasional, confused Frenchman can sometimes be spotted in the right season.

Before leaving this motley crew and heading into Beaubourg itself, walk down to the right-hand side of the building and take a look at the Stravinsky Fountain, an intriguing specimen of "clockwork" art. Down this side and along the back you will see the design element that has made Beaubourg such a controversial structure. All the pipes and ducts that carry the building's services are on the *outside,* brightly painted, instead of being inside and hidden.

The main entrance to Beaubourg is at the base of the slope of the square. Inside, you will find the central information desk and a good museum shop. On the left as you go in is the Salle d'Actualité. Choose a record and a seat, hand over the numbers, and you can listen to your record for as long as you like.

You are in one of the most popular buildings in Europe. Be prepared to stand in line for some time before even being allowed onto the escalator which will take you up to the exhibition floors—safety regulations do not allow more than 4,300 people in the building at any one time.

The principal attraction is the Modern Art Museum, housed on the top floor. It's intelligently arranged, and in every way a magnificent collection. The museum also presents a considerable number of temporary exhibits every year, many of them of the highest quality. But this is more than just a museum. It fulfills an important role as a place of learning and study, charting, and in some cases instituting, every twist and turn in the shifting, enormously complex, and mysterious world of contemporary art. It's a vital, living barometer of modern culture.

While one can unreservedly applaud Beaubourg's innovative and frequently challenging approach, what one thinks of the building in which this all takes place is a matter of taste. Like Les Halles, you'll love it or hate it!

Beaubourg is open Monday and Wednesday through Friday from 12 to 10 P.M. and Saturday and Sunday from 10 to 10 P.M. It's closed on Tuesday and free on Sunday morning. The nearest métro is Rambuteau.

THE MARAIS

Walk north around Beaubourg and take the rue Rambuteau east (buy yourself some tasty pastries, and croissants, or some fresh fruit, here). Turn left into the rue des Archives. You are now in the heart of the Marais.

On your right is the Hôtel de Soubise, 60 rue des Francs-Bourgeois, which, with its neighbor, the Hôtel de Rohan, houses the magnificent collection that is the **French Archives:** 280 kilometers—a staggering 175 miles—of shelving containing the wills of Louis XIV and Napoleon, the Declaration of the Rights of Man, letters from Voltaire and Joan of Arc, and much, much more. Both the museum and some of the sumptuously-decorated apartments can be visited. They're open Monday through Sunday—closed Tuesday—from 2 to 5. The Hôtel de Rohan is also closed in July and August. In June 1988 the Archives Nationales opened the **Caran,** at 11 rue des Quatre-Fils, a brand-new, fully computerized, concrete-and-smoked-glass building designed by architect Stanislas Fiszer. Here you can consult microfilm on the country's history for as long as you like. A yearly entrance card costs

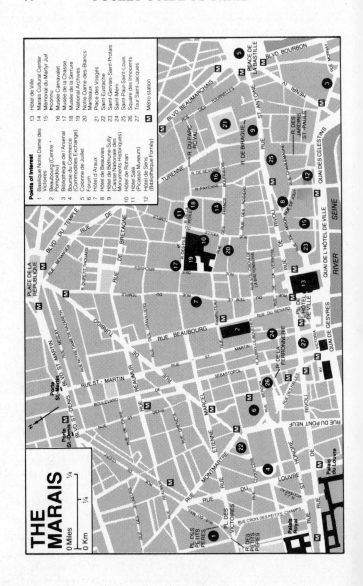

THE MARAIS

0 Miles 1/4

0 Km 1/4

Points of Interest

1 Basilique Notre Dame des Victoires
2 Beaubourg (Centre Pompidou)
3 Bibliothèque de l'Arsenal
4 Bourse du Commerce (Commodities Exchange)
5 Colonne de Juillet
6 Forum
7 Hôtel d'Avaux
8 Hôtel de Beauvais
9 Hôtel de Béthune Sully (Caisse Nationale des Monuments Historiques)
10 Hôtel de Rohan
11 Hôtel de Sens (Bibliothèque Forney)
12 Hôtel Salé (Picasso Museum)
13 Hôtel de Ville
14 Marais Cultural Center
15 Mémorial du Martyr Juif Inconnu
16 Musée Carnavalet
17 Musée de la Chasse
18 Musée de la Serrure
19 National Archives
20 Notre-Dame-des-Blancs-Manteaux
21 Place des Vosges
22 Saint-Eustache
23 Saint-Gervais-Saint-Protais
24 Saint-Merri
25 Saint-Paul-Saint-Louis
26 Square des Innocents
27 Tour Saint-Jacques

Ⓜ Métro station

100 frs. Take your passport. It's open daily year-round 9–6 except Saturday.

A little farther up the rue des Archives is the **Musée de la Chasse,** the Hunting Museum. The museum itself is only of secondary interest, but the building and formal garden are delightful. (Apply to the museum for permission to see the garden: tel. 42-72-86-43).

Go down the rue des 4 Fils and turn left into the rue de Thorigny. Here, housed in what was originally the Hôtel Salé, is the **Musée Picasso,** the first museum dedicated entirely to the maverick Spanish master, and, with Beaubourg and the Musée d'Orsay, one of Paris's top tourist attractions. The collection consists mainly of works Picasso kept for himself, but it's far from being just a series of sketches or false starts that he couldn't sell. Quite the opposite, in fact. It contains some superb works, including some very unusual sculptures, that for one reason or another Picasso refused to part with. In addition, Picasso's personal collection of paintings and drawings by friends and contemporaries—Braque, Matisse, Miró, and others—is also on show. The icing on the cake is provided by the building itself, a marvelous mid-17th century town house that took an astonishing ten years to restore. Don't miss it.

The museum, at 5 rue de Thorigny, is open daily, except Tuesday, from 9:15–5:15 (10 P.M. on Wednesday).

A few blocks south of the Musée Picasso is the **Musée Carnavalet,** at 23 rue de Sévigné. This, too, is a delightful building, with a collection illustrating every phase of Parisian history and architecture. Carnavalet's renowned collection of souvenirs from the 1789 Revolution was transferred to **Hôtel Le Peletier de St. Fargeau** down the road at #29 for the 1989 bicentenary celebrations. Meanwhile, recent renovations at Carnavalet have equipped it with a large workshop for children and a number of souvenir shops. It's open every day except Monday and public holidays from 10 to 5:40, and is free on Sundays.

From the Musée Carnavalet, head down the rue des Francs Bourgeois to the **place des Vosges,** a haven of trees, arcades, and elegant architecture. The square dates from the early 17th century, from the reign of Henri IV, at whose command it was laid out. #6 is today the **Musée Victor Hugo,** full of memorabilia of the great French writer. It's open every day (except Monday) from 10 to 5:30. For a good cup of coffee and a bite to eat, try **Ma Bourgogne** in the northwest corner of the square. Meals are served all day long.

Head south out of the place des Vosges, and turn right into the rue St.-Antoine. A block or two along, turn right up the little rue Pavée. This brings you to the rue des Rosiers and the **Jewish quarter.** Although the district is superficially down at heel, the true heart of the Marais continues to beat in its narrow streets. It is lined with Hebrew signs hanging over tiny food shops, bookshops and restaurant-cum-delicatessens like **Jo Goldenberg's** at #7, the scene of a tragic massacre is 1982. There are several superb baker's shops that are packed on Sunday afternoons. Try the strudel with hazelnuts at **Korcarz** (#29).

Head over the rue de Rivoli to the **Hôtel de Ville,** the City Hall, in the place de l'Hôtel de Ville. The building is a 19th-century copy of the original 16th-century building—this was burned down during the Commune in 1871—and the seat of the city government. Inside there's a veritable feast of extravagant painting and decoration. It's open Monday to Friday 9–6:30, and Saturday 9 to 6. There are guided tours of the salons on Mondays at 10:30. Reservations necessary (tel. 42–76–43–43).

The Ile St.-Louis and Ile de la Cité

Begin with the **Ile St.-Louis,** smaller of the two islands in the Seine. Predominantly residential, it is a delightful place to stroll, either along the quays or down the rue St. Louis-en-l'Ile that runs through the center. Here you will find the church of the same name, a number of good shops and restaurants, and, at #31, **Berthillon,** *the* ice cream shop. You can't possibly try all the flavors, but cram in as many as you can manage. If necessary, come back every day. They also supply little boxes in which the ice cream will last at least as long as it takes to go to the Tuileries on foot. (There's a chance that Berthillon's ice cream, securely packed in one of their little boxes, might make it to New York by Concorde, if the traffic to Paris airport isn't too bad.) Berthillon ice cream can also be found now in most of the cafés on the island.

If you prefer tea, there is the **Salon du Thé St.-Louis** at #81, and, if you prefer beer, there is the **Brasserie de l'Ile St.-Louis** beside the Pont St.-Louis. Nearby are some magnificent patisserie shops.

To get to the **Ile de la Cité,** cross over the little Pont St.-Louis at the west end of the Ile St.-Louis. Here you will find much more bustle, and much more to see. To put it another way, this is a place for serious sightseeing.

The three principal attractions on the Ile de la Cité are Notre Dame, the Conciergerie, and the Sainte-Chapelle. These are buildings that overawe through their sheer scale, and historical and architectural grandeur. They are somber, beautiful, magnificent, and unforgettable. This is as it should be, for you are now in the very heart of the city. Mind you, you won't be alone, for the Ile de la Cité draws tourists in much the same way as the Beaubourg or the Eiffel Tower.

Notre Dame dates from 1163, and was largely complete by 1250. Most of the sculptures on the facade are 19th-century replicas, many of the originals—particularly those representing the 28 kings of Israel—having been hacked down in the Revolution when they were erroneously identified with the French royal family. (Similarly, the spire, or *flèche,* over the chancel was also added in the last century). The three doorways are, from left to right, the Portal of the Virgin (the central sculpture here, the Virgin and Child, *is* original, and dates from the 13th century), the Portal of the Last Judgement, and the Portal of St.-Anne. Above them is one of the cathedral's three famous rose windows. To bask in the shimmering pools of light and color it creates, step inside the building.

The massive 12th-century columns of the nave stretch away from you to the transepts—the "arms" of the church—and the chancel, or choir. A good part of the glass in the fabulous rose windows of the transepts is original. The chancel owes much of its appearance to a vow made by Louis XIII in 1638. Childless after 23 years of marriage, he promised to dedicate the whole of France to the Virgin Mary if his queen provided an heir. An heir was duly produced, and the king, by way of thanks, had statues of himself and his son—the future Louis XIV—placed in the chancel, as well as new choir stalls. To the south of the choir is the old sacristy, now the treasury, with a display of chalices and other ecclesiastical objects and manuscripts. Open 10–6 (2–6 on Sunday); 15 frs.

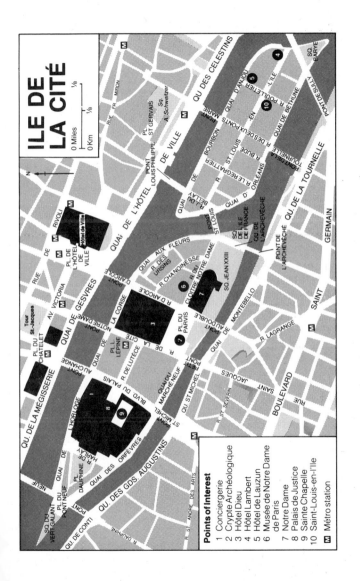

ILE DE LA CITÉ

Points of Interest

1 Conciergerie
2 Crypte Archéologique
3 Hôtel Dieu
4 Hôtel Lambert
5 Hôtel de Lauzun
6 Musée de Notre Dame de Paris
7 Notre Dame
8 Palais de Justice
9 Sainte Chapelle
10 Saint-Louis-en-l'Ile

Ⓜ Métro station

There is also a nail and a splinter of wood, reputedly from the True Cross. These are produced on Sundays in Lent and on Good Friday.

If you're feeling hale and hearty, make your way to the north aisle near the Portal of the Virgin and climb the 387 steps to the summit of the north tower. From here, in the company of a series of grotesque gargoyles and other carved monsters, including the famous "striga" or vampire, who, chin in hands, passively contemplates the city's roof tops, you can cross over to the south tower. Visit the 13-ton bell here. It's still rung on special occasions. Towers open 10–5; 22 frs.

At the west end of the Ile de la Cité is the **Palais de Justice,** the city law courts. It's open to the public so you can wander around the corridors watching the important-seeming bustle of the law-givers, or even attend a court hearing. But the major points of interest here are the Sainte-Chapelle and the Conciergerie.

The **Sainte-Chapelle,** hidden inside a courtyard of the Palais de Justice, is a stunning jewel case of a building. It was put up by Louis IX, otherwise known as Saint Louis (the genial and pious monarch was canonized 27 years after his death). Having purchased what he took to be the original Crown of Thorns from the Emperor Baldwin II of Constantinople, Louis resolved that a suitable shrine should be built to house it. The Sainte-Chapelle, completed in 1248—airy and diaphanous, glowing with light from its sensational stained glass—was the result. The lower half is somewhat gloomy these days, but the upper chapel remains among the city's most precious treasures. To see it at its most magnificent you should try to attend one of the candlelit concerts held at frequent intervals.

The Sainte-Chapelle is open every day from 10–5.

The fairytale towers of the **Conciergerie** are best seen from the Quai de la Mégisserie across the Seine or, when lit up at night, from the Right Bank expressway through Paris. But, the history of this one-time prison reads more like a horror story than a fairytale. The **Bonbec** tower, which is the oldest and on the right if you're looking from across the river, was the setting for interrogations and torture for centuries. Marie-Antoinette, Robespierre, and Danton were among the famous prisoners awaiting execution in the cells of the Conciergerie. In 1988 the cells were closed for "renovations" in preparation for the French Revolution's bicentenary celebrations, and re-opened in April '89. The name of the building derives from the fact that it was originally presided over by the governor, or concierge, of the royal palace. His considerable income was greatly increased by the special privilege he enjoyed of leasing out the shops and showrooms that once lined the first floor. The most distinctive features of the building are its four towers overlooking the Seine, the most famous of which is the Tour de l'Horloge, the Clock Tower, on the corner of the boulevard du Palais. The clock itself has been ticking away since 1370, and is the oldest public clock in the city.

You'll have to take a tour if you want to visit the inside, but it's well worth it. The splendid guardroom, with Gothic vaulting and columns decorated with intricately-carved capitals, and the huge Salle des Gens d'Armes are among the highlights. But you can also see the prisoners' gallery and the chapel. Highlifers should note that the kitchens, boasting four of the largest fireplaces you're likely to encounter anywhere, can be rented out should you have a yen to throw a really memorable party.

The Ile de la Cité has no shortage of tourist-type cafés and restaurants where you can get a moderately good bite to eat. Among the best are the **Caveau du Palais** (#19) and **Chez Paul** (#15), both on the place Dauphine at the western end of the island overlooking the river.

The Left Bank

Begin your exploration of the Left Bank at the northern end of the boulevard St.-Michel, opposite the Ile de la Cité, by the Pont St.-Michel. This is the Latin Quarter. The name comes from the fact that this area of the city has long been the student quarter. As Latin remained the official language of education right up to the Revolution, so the area got its name. Head south down the boulevard St.-Michel, past the many bookshops and cafés, to the boulevard St.-Germain. To your right is St.-Germain itself; to your left the **Musée de Cluny.** Make a bee line for the museum.

It's housed in one of the few medieval houses—as opposed to public or religious buildings—left in the city. It was built for the monks of the rich and influential Cluny Abbey in Burgundy as their Paris HQ. Intriguingly, it stands on the site of the city's original Roman baths, impressive sections of which can be seen. The museum has a fine collection of medieval arts—statuary, jewelry, furniture, religious artifacts—the pearl in the collection being the superb *Dame à la Licorne* tapestries, a highly allegorical, late-medieval series of tapestries whose exact meaning has long since been lost. Their curious ambiguity only makes them all the more appealing. The museum also contains a number of the original 13th-century statues from the facade of Notre Dame. The museum is open daily, except Tuesday, from 9:45 to 12:30, and 2 to 5:15. Half price on Sunday and public holidays.

Leaving the Musée de Cluny, you'll see the gray bulk of the **Sorbonne** in front of you, the city's principal university building. It was founded by one Robert de Sorbon, from whom it takes its name.

Behind the Sorbonne head up the rue St.-Jacques to the forbidding mausoleum called the **Panthéon.** Beneath its vast dome are buried such illuminati as Voltaire, Rousseau, and Victor Hugo. This spendidly gloomy classical structure also contains a number of interesting Late 19th-century murals by Puvis de Chavannes, the most famous of which illustrates the story of Ste.-Geneviève, patron saint of Paris, and one-time shepherdess. The Panthéon is open every day from 10–12 and 2–5.

You can make a substantial detour from here if you like plants and animals. This is to the **Jardin des Plantes,** the botanical gardens, about half a mile to the east of the Panthéon. Despite an excellent Natural History museum and a charming, decidedly old-fashioned zoo, the gardens are not on the tourist's beaten path, but they are worth a quiet visit. The museum is open 2–5; closed Tuesday.

From the Panthéon, back again on our main route, walk down the rue Soufflot to the boulevard St.-Michel, which here runs down past the **Jardin du Luxembourg.** There is a cluster of little cafés and restaurants where, for the price of no more than a cup of coffee, you can sit for hours and watch the endless procession of people up and down the boulevard St.-Michel.

The gardens of the **Luxembourg Palace** are delightful, an oasis of greenery among the traffic-thronged streets. The Palace itself was built by Marie de Médicis, who, born and raised in Florence's Pitti Palace, intended it to resemble her childhood home. After serving as a prison in the Revolution, it became in turn the seat of the Directory and the Consulate. Today it is the Senate, France's Upper Chamber. There is, however, little of interest inside, and it is now closed to visitors. The gardens, with their Punch and Judy shows, fountains, and statues, are very much more diverting.

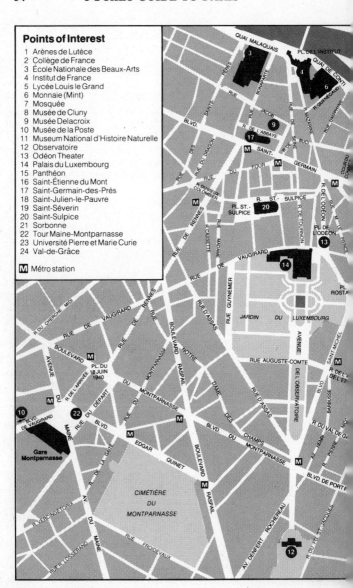

Points of Interest

1 Arènes de Lutèce
2 Collège de France
3 École Nationale des Beaux-Arts
4 Institut de France
5 Lycée Louis le Grand
6 Monnaie (Mint)
7 Mosquée
8 Musée de Cluny
9 Musée Delacroix
10 Musée de la Poste
11 Museum National d'Histoire Naturelle
12 Observatoire
13 Odéon Theater
14 Palais du Luxembourg
15 Panthéon
16 Saint-Étienne du Mont
17 Saint-Germain-des-Prés
18 Saint-Julien-le-Pauvre
19 Saint-Séverin
20 Saint-Sulpice
21 Sorbonne
22 Tour Maine-Montparnasse
23 Université Pierre et Marie Curie
24 Val-de-Grâce

Ⓜ Métro station

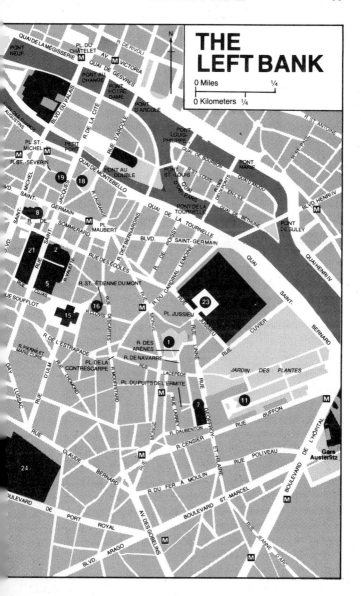

The southern end of the gardens leads to the **Paris observatory,** where, on the first Sunday of each month at 2:30 in the afternoon, you can contemplate the cosmos (apply in writing to the Secretary, L'Observatoire, 61 avenue de l'Observatoire, 14e, or tel. 40-51-22-21).

From here, if you still have any energy left—the area is liberally provided with restaurants, cafés, and bars for those in need of refreshment—a side trip to Montparnasse is in order. You can either walk up the boulevard du Montparnasse or take the métro to the aptly named Montparnasse-Bienvenüe station.

Montparnasse has long been known chiefly as a district of poets and painters. Today, however, it is an area of towering skyscrapers and large modern hotels. But don't despair, the old Montparnasse is still there, struggling to survive and well worth seeking out. You'll never be short of entertainment, with movie theaters, café-theaters, and all the famous bars and cafés—of which more in a moment—still very much in evidence.

Begin your visit in the place du 18 Juin 1940. Its curious name commemorates the date of de Gaulle's famous radio appeal to all Frenchmen, broadcast from London just after the fall of France. Towering over the square is the **Tour Maine-Montparnasse,** a dull hulk of steel and concrete, all 59 stories of it. It also has what is claimed to be the fastest elevator in Europe, which is well worth taking for the amazing view of the city. The building's open every day from 9:30 A.M. to 11 P.M. It will cost you 32 frs. to ride to the top and 25.50 frs. to the snack bar and cafeteria on floor 56. Children 5–14 pay 19 and 12.50 frs. respectively; children under 5 ride free.

At its base is the Commercial Shopping Center, a substantial modern mall that includes a branch of the famous Galeries Lafayette department store.

But if, like most visitors to Montparnasse, it's a spot of relaxed entertainment that has drawn you, head for the rue de la Gaîté. It's been crammed with dance halls, theaters, night-clubs, and restaurants since the 18th century. Inevitably perhaps, though it's not nearly as bad as **Pigalle** away to the north of the city, there's a degree of sleaze among the glamor, so be on your guard.

Alternatively, back on the boulevard du Montparnasse, you'll find the **Dôme** and the **Coupole,** both substantial café/brasseries, once the haunt of Hemingway, Joyce, Modigliani, Pound, Cocteau, and a whole host of lesser poets and painters earlier this century when Paris really was the artistic capital of the world. Among the supporting cast of thousands in those days was Lenin, too, though it's hard to imagine that he added much to the fun. At the far end of the boulevard du Montparnasse is the romantically named **Closerie des Lilas.** Today it's principally just a rather expensive restaurant, but you can still have a drink here and dream of the days when this pretty spot was a center of bohemianism à la Parisienne.

ST.-GERMAIN

St.-Germain is north of the Palais de Luxembourg and west of the boulevard St.-Michel. It's a haunt of artists, intellectuals, and writers rather than a sightseeing area as such. Only the two churches of **St.-Germain-des-Prés,** the only Romanesque or pre-Gothic church in the city (apart from St.-Pierre atop Montmartre) and **St.-Sulpice,** famed for its Delacroix murals and a fine organ, are liable to figure on the tourist's checklist. But St.-Germain itself is a marvelous area to wander around. It's busy, colorful, and cosmopolitan, with an accumulation of "in"cafés, restaurants, and bars among immaculate high-fashion shops and elegant buildings. The cafés **Flore, Aux Deux Magots,** and **Bonaparte** around the place St.-Germain and **Lipp** on the busy boulevard St.-Germain have all remained distinctly elegant and sophisticated.

The little streets to the north of the boulevard St.-Germain—the rue Jacob, the rue Bonaparte, the rue de Seine, and the rue de Mazarine—are packed with restaurants, food shops (there's a particularly good food market in the rue de Buci), and art galleries. There's an indefinably Gallic quality about the whole area. It's unmistakably chic; it's crammed full of excellent restaurants; and it's full of unexpected nooks and crannies revealing hidden treasures. One such is in the place Fürstemberg, a little square just off the rue Jacob. Here the 19th-century painter Delacroix had his studio, which has been turned into a charming little museum, the **Musée Eugène Delacroix** (open daily except Tuesday from 9:45 to 12:30 and 2 to 5:15).

Anyone hoping to break away from the beaten path of mass tourism should seriously consider staying in this area—see 6th Arrondissement in the Hotel listings for details. For a combination of charm, character, and convenience—it is, after all, very central—St.-Germain is hard to beat.

THE MUSEE d'ORSAY

The newest museum in Paris, the **Musée d'Orsay,** opened at the end of 1986 and immediately became one of the city's most popular attractions. To reach it from St.-Germain, follow the rue Jacob westward, continue along the rue de l'Université, then turn right towards the river on rue Bellechasse.

The Musée d'Orsay, like so many Parisian museums, is fascinating as a building in its own right. It was built as a rail station in the late 1890s, but had only a short working life. Electrification of the railways created longer trains that wouldn't fit under the great arched roof. The station was saved from demolition in 1978 by being classified as an historical monument, legislation which paved the way for its transformation into a museum to house fine and applied arts—mainly French—from the period 1848–1914.

The huge job of converting the interior was given to an Italian architect, Gae Aulenti, who divided the building into three main areas: the soaring space under the old station roof; the splendid public rooms of the former hotel that run down one side of the complex; and the rooms on the upper floors of the hotel. She created what looks like the bottom half of a De Mille film set, built out of limestone, to fill the area where the tracks used to run. The art on display here is massive, with acres of canvas and tons of stone, while more intimate pieces can be seen in the surrounding maze of small walled areas.

The middle level, partly in the old hotel, is a glorious mixture of paintings, furniture, sculpture, china, and glass, a lot of it Art Nouveau. One of the highlights is part of the original building, the Salle des Fêtes, a faithfully restored Belle Epoque room with crystal swags and mirrors. On the floor above are the Impressionists and other late-1800s artists. There are pictures here known across the world—works by Manet, Monet, Renoir, Degas, Van Gogh, Cézanne, Degas,

Toulouse Lautrec, and others. If these are painters who interest you, arrive early in the day and head directly to these rooms. Later in the day, it's almost impossible to get near the works of art you want to see. Up here, too, you can look out across the Seine to the Tuileries garden through the glass face of one of the two great clocks.

There is a rooftop café and a restaurant, but there are always long lines around lunchtime. Indeed, it's almost impossible to get into the restaurant without a reservation. The area around the museum has plenty of quiet places to eat that can take up the overflow.

The museum is open 10 to 6 (Thursday 10 to 9:45); closed Monday.

THE MUSEE RODIN AND
THE INVALIDES

Return to the rue Bellechasse when you leave the museum, walk away from the river, cross the boulevard St.-Germain, and then turn right on to the rue de Varenne. You will have been walking through the heart of French bureaucracy, for these streets contain many government offices, among them the Ministry of Education, the Ministry of Industry, and the Ministry of Agriculture.

On the lefthand side of the rue de Varenne, at the very end, is the **Musée Rodin** (also called the Hôtel Biron), nestling in a big garden. This attractive old house was once the home and studio of France's greatest sculptor, some of whose work you will just have seen at Orsay. There is lots more of it here. The rooms are full of pieces at every stage of evolution, as well as his working sketches. You can relax in the gardens, which are especially pretty in late spring and summer. Some of the most important sculptures have been set out under the trees.

The Hôtel Biron is open daily, except Monday, 10 to 6, last entry 5:45 (5, October through February); half price on Sunday.

Across the road from the Musée Rodin is the symbolic core of the French obsession with Glory, the tomb of Napoleon and the **Musée de l'Armée** (the Army Museum) in the **Hôtel des Invalides.** The museum is so well planned, and so full of fascinating historical exhibits, that it should grip even those who aren't normally interested in military things. Behind the museum is the great Church of the Dome, the vast structure that guards Napoleon's red porphyry tomb. The setting was designed with an eye to giving the little Emperor the kind of theatrical grandeur in death that he strove for in life. The tomb is sunk into a circular crypt, so that you can look down on it. You can also descend to the level of the crypt for a closer view. Between the huge, domed mausoleum and the museum lies the Church of **St. Louis des Invalides,** hung with tattered flags, captured from France's enemies. There is a *Son et Lumière* show telling the story of the return to Paris of Napoleon's remains from St. Helena, the lonely Atlantic island where the Emperor passed his last unhappy days. It is given twice nightly, once in English and once in French.

The museum is open daily 10 to 5 (to 6, April through September). The tomb may be visited up to 7 all year; closed on most public holidays.

From the place Vauban, behind the Church of the Dome, turn right along avenue de Tourville, then left to reach the southern end of the Champ de Mars, a long orderly park which leads straight back to the Seine and the Eiffel Tower, where your tour began.

Hotels

Finding the right hotel in Paris is easy. The city is full of places to stay in all price categories. Prices are not always low—at the top end of the scale there's practically no limit to how much you can pay—but you will usually get value for money. The French have a real flair for running hotels, and have long since mastered the art of combining comfort and efficiency.

There are some practical points to bear in mind. First, book ahead. Parisian hotels, especially the better ones, tend to be booked up some time in advance, whether by delegates attending one of the many trade fairs or by tourists. You can book through your travel agent or direct with the hotel. Alternatively, try *Commercialisation Hôtelière & Touristique,* 42 rue le Peletier, 75009 Paris (tel. 42-80-18-53). In the U.S., call them toll-free at 800–327–5118/432–1362 (telex 283 645 F). Second, French hotels charge by the room, not per person, a thoroughly sensible system. Most rooms are doubles. The few single ones left tend to be pokey and on a top floor. Third, a *salle de bain,* whatever your school French may tell you, could be just a shower (if you want a real soaking tub you have to ask for a *baignoire*). Fourth, only the expensive hotels will have air-conditioning, so, if the hotel you choose is on a noisy street, ask for a room *sur cour* (many hotels are built round a courtyard), or away from the street. Fifth, the French, perhaps with memories of the guillotine, often sleep with a torture device like a solid sausage, called a *traversin,* an old-fashioned bolster. If you want a restful night, ask for *oreillers,* pillows.

Apartments can be rented from *Paris-Séjour Réservation,* 90 ave. des Champs-Elysées, 8e (tel. 42-56-30-00) or *Paris Bienvenue,* 10 ave. de Vilars, 7e (tel. 47-53-80-81).

We have arranged the following hotels by arrondissement, covering the central ones only.

FIRST ARRONDISSEMENT

Family Hotel, 35 rue Cambon (tel. 42-61-54-84). A small inexpensive hotel with extremely friendly atmosphere. It can be a real pleasure to stay here. All the rooms have bathrooms.

Londres Stockholm, 13 rue St.-Roch (tel. 42-60-15-62). 28 rooms, 26 with bath or shower. Moderately priced, and very conveniently located near the Palais Royal and the Tuileries Gardens.

Normandy, 7 rue de l'Echelle (tel. 42-60-30-21). 140 rooms, all with bath. A comfortable hotel, attractively decorated. There's a good restaurant, plus a relaxing, wood-paneled bar. Excellent location just north of the rue du Rivoli and the Tuileries Gardens. Rates are moderate.

Palais, 2 quai de la Mégisserie (tel. 42-36-98-25). 19 rooms, a few with bath or shower. A modest hotel, but the low rates and the excellent location on the Ile de la Cité, opposite the Sainte-Chapelle, make it a worthwhile bet.

Ritz, 15 pl. Vendôme (tel. 42-60-38-30). 187 rooms and suites. This is one of the top hotels in Paris, indeed in Europe, offering an equal measure of superb old-world charm and service, and every modern facility, with prices to match. It's owned by the same Egyptian family that now own Harrods in London. They have spared no expense in inaugurating a lavish program of restoration and redevelopment. In 1988 they opened a vast health complex with a gym, sauna, turkish baths and squash court. There are two magnificent restaurants, including *L'Espadon,* two small but renowned bars, a pretty courtyard garden, a swimming-pool, and air-conditioning throughout.

SECOND ARRONDISSEMENT

Choiseul-Opéra, 1 rue Daunou (tel. 42-61-70-41). 43 rooms, all with bath or shower. Excellent location on the same street as the celebrated Harry's Bar, and very close to the Opéra. Moderately priced.

Edouard-VII, 39 av. de l'Opéra (tel. 42-61-56-90). 100 rooms, all with bath or shower. Luxurious spot by the Opéra. The restaurant here, the *Delmonico,* is highly recommended.

L'Horset Opéra d'Antin, 18 rue d'Antin (tel. 47-42-13-01). 60 rooms, 52 with shower. This hotel, expensive if not absolutely in the top bracket, is a member of the well-run Horset chain. However, it's the central location, just off the avenue de l'Opéra, that makes it worth trying, especially for shoppers.

Westminster, 13 rue de la Paix (tel. 42-61-57-46). 102 rooms, all with bath or shower. Restaurant, air-conditioning, and splendid location just off the place Vendôme single out this old favorite. It has recently been completely renovated. Prices are high, but justified.

THIRD ARRONDISSEMENT

Pavillon de la Reine, 28 place des Vosges (tel. 42-77-96-40). 50 rooms and suites, all with bath. This opened in 1986 and quickly became very popular, partly because of its location—the entrance is on the beautiful place des Vosges—but also because of its tastefully decorated rooms and duplexes, with their marble bathrooms and views over the square or the flower-filled patio. Breakfast is served in a vaulted cellar. Private garage; no restaurant. Luxury to Expensive category.

FOURTH ARRONDISSEMENT

Bretonnerie, 22 rue Ste.-Croix-de-la-Bretonnerie (tel. 48-87-77-63). 32 rooms, all with bath or shower. Charming 17th-century building near the Hôtel de Ville, Beaubourg, and the Marais. Antiques decorate some of the rooms, and there's a good bar. Prices are moderate.

Deux-Iles, 59 rue St.-Louis-en-l'Ile (tel. 43-26-13-35). 17 rooms, all with bath or shower. An attractive small hotel on the residential and elegant Ile St.-Louis; located in a fine 17th-century building. There's a bar and a sitting room in the old cellars. All in all, an excellent deal, especially in view of the less than astronomic prices.

Lutèce, 65 rue St.-Louis-en-l'Ile (tel. 43-26-23-52). 23 rooms, all with bath or shower. A quiet and comfortable hotel in an historic building. It belongs to the same owners as the Deux-Iles (above) and you'll get the same friendly welcome. Small—some rooms *very* small—and attractive, with reasonable rates. Ask for a room under the eaves for a view over the rooftops and the Panthéon. Residents are welcome at the Deux Iles' bar.

Saint-Louis, 75 rue St.-Louis-en-l'Ile (tel. 46-34-04-80). 21 rooms, all with bath. This is an attractive hotel, offering very good value. Tremendous views from the top story. And peace and quiet comes as standard.

FIFTH ARRONDISSEMENT

Avenir, 52 rue Gay-Lussac (tel. 43-54-76-60). 44 rooms, only 10 with bath or shower. A modest hotel with very low prices. On six floors, with no elevator.

Colbert, 7 rue de l'Hôtel Colbert (tel. 43-25-85-65). 40 rooms, all with bath or shower. Close to the Seine, just opposite Notre Dame. Attractive, if slightly small rooms, in an 18th-century building. Comfortable. Prices are high.

Esmeralda, 4 rue St.-Julien-le-Pauvre (tel. 43-54-19-20). 19 rooms, 15 with bath or shower. Very pretty 17th-century building by the attractive square Viviani, just opposite Notre Dame, on the Left Bank. The rooms are smallish, but well furnished, and rates moderate.

Grandes Ecoles, 75 rue Cardinal-Lemoine (tel. 43-26-79-23). The countryside in the heart of Paris. This charming little hotel, tucked at the end of a private alleyway, is an old house with trellised roses growing outside and a small colonnaded garden. The bedrooms are small and simple, but just right, and prices low. Book early.

SIXTH ARRONDISSEMENT

L'Abbaye Saint-Germain, 10 rue Cassette (tel. 45-44-38-11). 45 rooms, all with bath or shower. Originally an abbey—with paved garden and pleasant courtyard to prove it—this is a distinctly discriminating spot in the heart of literary St.-Germain. It's fairly expensive, and you must book well in advance—especially for a first-floor courtyard room—but it's very welcoming.

Angleterre, 44 rue Jacob (tel. 42-60-34-72). 30 rooms, all with bath or shower. Still exuding the atmosphere of a plush private house (it was once the home of the British Ambassador), this is a delightful hotel; excellently-run, with extremely comfortable rooms, some luxurious bathrooms and a pretty courtyard. And all in the heart of St.-Germain. Unbeatable value.

L'Hôtel, 13 rue des Beaux Arts (tel. 43-25-27-22). 27 rooms, all with bath. This is one of the rare super-deluxe hotels on the Left Bank and is quite unlike anything else in the city. It's very small, very, very chic (Mick Jagger's a regular), and very expensive. If you're lucky you may even get the room where Oscar Wilde died in 1900.

La Louisiane, 60 rue de Seine (tel. 43-29-59-30). Book early; this place fills up with journalists and Italian models. It's a two-star place, so not too expensive, if somewhat self-consciously simple. It was originally a private home, and long famous as the haunt of Hemingway and Sartre. Can be a bit noisy, so ask for the quieter rooms.

Lutétia, 45 blvd. Raspail (tel. 45-44-38-10). 300 rooms, all with bath or shower. Near the Bon Marché department store, with an attractive atmosphere and good, old-fashioned service. Renovated from top to toe in the mid '80s under the eagle eye of fashion designer Sonia Rykiel. She's produced a supremely elegant modern Art Deco palace. Restaurant and bar too. Expensive.

Saints-Pères, 65 rue des Saints-Pères (tel. 45-44-50-00). 37 rooms, all with bath or shower. There's everything here you could want: space, style, and silence (especially in rooms that overlook the gardens), plus a touch of modernity. The mezzanine apartments under the rafters are exclusively for newlyweds and have a perfect garden view. Suprisingly low rates.

Vieux Paris, 9 rue Gît-le-Coeur (tel. 43-54-41-66). 21 rooms, 10 with bath or shower. On a picturesque street close to the river and the place St.-Michel. Friendly service, low rates, lots of charm, and an old building produce a winning combination.

SEVENTH ARRONDISSEMENT

Pont-Royal, 7 rue Montalembert (tel. 45-44-38-27). 78 rooms, all with bath or shower. Near the new Orsay Museum. Some of the rooms are cramped considering the deluxe prices, but the atmosphere is attractive and welcoming. There's a good bar and restaurant, and air-conditioning.

Résidence Elysées-Maubourg, 35 blvd. de Latour-Maubourg (tel. 45-56-10-78). 30 rooms, all with bath or shower. An older building, extensively modernized in the mid '80s. Though small, it's very comfortable. Close to Les Invalides and the Eiffel Tower.

Varenne, 44 rue de Bourgogne (tel. 45-51-45-55). 24 rooms, all with bath or shower. A peaceful and friendly one-time private mansion, with a pretty little patio. Very good value for the moderate rates.

Verneuil St.-Germain, 8 rue de Verneuil (tel. 42-60-24-16). 26 rooms, all with bath or shower. A cosy modern hotel, with all amenities—plus beams, stylish wallpaper, and fabrics—on a quiet street. The accent here is very much on charm. Prices are low for what's offered.

EIGHTH ARRONDISSEMENT

Bristol, 112 fbg. St.-Honoré (tel. 42-66-91-45). 200 rooms and suites. One of the most elegant—and expensive—hotels in the city. Close to the British Embassy and just a stone's throw from the Elysée Palace, it's in the throbbing heart of chic Paris. Luxury abounds. There's also an excellent restaurant, and a rooftop swimming-pool.

Chambiges, 8 rue Chambiges (tel. 47-23-80-49). 30 rooms, 22 with bath or shower. Pleasant and modest little hotel close to the Seine and the avenue Montaigne. There are a few more expensive rooms, but rates are otherwise moderate.

Crillon, 10 pl. de la Concorde (tel. 42-65-24-24). 189 rooms. The grandiose site, with views over the place de la Concorde to the National Assembly, and building have long since made this super deluxe hotel an institution. It's a regular stopping off point for top Americans, and has been since Benjamin Franklin and Thomas Jefferson stayed here when it was a private palace. A thorough renovation in the early '80s has kept it comfortable and ultra smart. It also boasts just about the best hotel restaurant—*Les Ambassadeurs*—in the city.

George V, 31 av. George V (tel. 47-23-54-00). 292 rooms. Located close to the Champs-Elysées, this ultra-fashionable haunt is popular with oil sheiks, movie stars, businessmen, and mere millionaires alike. The bar is almost a club for those who pull the strings that count. Every facility you can think of, and a few more beside.

Lancaster, 7 rue de Berri (tel. 43-59-90-43). 67 rooms, all with bath. Luxury, exclusivity, and impeccable service single out the Lancaster as a quite phenomenally good hotel. The furnishings are magnificent, the restaurant excellent, and there's a charming little garden. The location, just off the Champs Elysées and close to the Arc de Triomphe, is equally desirable.

Roblin, 6 rue Chauveau-Lagarde (tel. 42-65-57-00). 67 rooms, 62 with bath or shower. Well-placed near the Madeleine and good for serious shoppers: The Faubourg St.-Honoré and the big department stores are all close at hand. Good restaurant—*Le Mazagran* (closed August and weekends)—and bar. Fairly expensive, but not bank-breakingly so.

Le Tremoille, 14 rue de la Tremoille (tel. 47-23-34-20). 111 rooms, all with bath or shower. Good service, all modern facilities, and period furnishings. Prices are high, but value is good. Near the Champs-Elysées and the *couture* houses (popular with top models and their escorts).

Restaurants

Food is more than just important to the French. It is a way of life, an art form, an indispensable part of being. In recent years the French Government has officially recognized the Art and Science of French Cuisine, and awarded a sizeable grant for its study, research, promotion, and practice. Figures such as Michel Guérard, Paul Bocuse, the Troisgros brothers, Michel Oliver and his son Raymond, Jean-Claude Bucher, Alain Senderens, and Roger Vergé are more than just household names: They are almost demi-gods.

There is a staggering wealth of riches from which to choose, from tiny, neighborhood cafés and bistros to the plushest temples of gastronomic delight, with just about everything in between: *cuisine bourgeoise, nouvelle cuisine, cuisine régionale,* even, for the desperate, Burger King. If you are after a complete, formal dinner, then *grande cuisine* is the one. If you prefer a simpler touch, yet still with a recognizably traditional twist, try *cuisine bourgeoise.* For an even lighter approach, with pure flavors, freshness, and an imaginative combination of ingredients, go for *nouvelle cuisine*. This is often prettily served, but in minuscule portions; and there's a saying that this style means less on the plate but more on the check. *Cuisine régionale* in Paris is excellent, marked by an enormous variety of traditional and specifically regional ingredients, and much ingenuity. There are also countless ethnic restaurants in the city, ranging from Chinese, Vietnamese, Japanese, Russian, and Kosher to Algerian, Moroccan, and Tunisian, with a handful of Indian and Indonesian haunts thrown in for good measure.

A word about prices: Parisian restaurants still offer generally good value for money. Catering to such a discriminating clientele, the city's restauranteurs keep prices low and offer value for money or go out of business faster than you can say *Garçon!* Most of the places we recommend here are not, therefore, excessively expensive, though where they are more expensive than the norm we say so (as we do for the really inexpensive places). But always make a point of checking the menu posted outside before you go in. If you think it unreasonable, go elsewhere. You'll never have trouble finding a substitute: Paris is a city of restaurants. You should also be sure to check the credit card stickers in the window. Don't assume that all the major cards will be accepted, because they won't.

If you are watching your dollars carefully, then be sure to check out the set menus (*menu* in French—an *à la carte* menu is a different animal). Many restaurants have several at different prices. The ones with especially interesting cuisine may have a gourmet *menu*. This will allow you to taste several of the chef's specialties at much less than if you had ordered them as separate dishes.

A final word of warning: Parisian restaurants have very variable opening times. A good many close for all or part of July and (especially) August. Many close on Monday, Sunday and public holidays. Always check before turning up.

No guide could ever do justice to the restaurants of Paris. Even the most comprehensive can present no more than the tip of the iceberg. The restaurants listed here, arranged by arrondissement, represent a mélange of the tried, the tested and the novel. But for every one we recommend there are probably another 20 just as good. Never be afraid to experiment. *Bon appétit!*

FIRST ARRONDISSEMENT

L'Absinthe, 24 place du Marché St.-Honoré (tel. 42-60-02-45). Friendly service in this chic little restaurant, close to place Vendôme and the avenue de l'Opéra. The cooking is original, with delectably fresh ingredients. Attractive decor with Art Nouveau bits and pieces. Closed Saturday for lunch, and Sunday.

Barrière Poquelin, 17 rue Molière (tel. 42-96-22-19). This is an intimate little restaurant near the Comédie Française and Palais Royal, with decor inspired by Molière's 18th-century plays. Chef/owner M. Gaullaumin serves original fish dishes, a range of game and a good-value fixed-price menu at lunch and dinner. Closed Saturday lunch, Sunday and first two weeks in August.

Le Carré des Feuillants, 14 rue de Castiglione (tel. 42-86-82-82). Anyone with pretensions to be numbered among *le beau monde* will already know that this elegant new restaurant offers one of the city's most talked about gastronomic experiences. Try for a table in the largest of the three dining rooms: there's a terrific fireplace. The food is predominantly from southwestern France, one of the richest gastronomic regions of the country. Foie gras, truffles and young pigeon are among the specialties and the wine list is fabulous. Expensive, but worth it. Closed Saturday lunch and Sunday (all weekend in July and August).

Bistro de la Gare, 30 rue St.-Denis (tel. 40-26-82-80). One of five similar restaurants run by Michel Oliver. Good, reliable food, with a special speedy service for theater-goers, at very reasonable prices. The restaurant is open every day of the year, with last orders at around midnight.

Le Grand Véfour, 17 rue de Beaujolais (tel. 42-96-56-27). The fact that two weeks is the minimum time you have to book ahead to get in here, and even then there's no guarantee of success, underlines only too clearly that this is one of the great gastronomic experiences Paris has to offer. Excellent food, superb service. Need we say more?

Mercure Galant, 15 rue des Petits Champs (tel. 42-97-53-85). A charmingly elegant Parisian house with fine *fin de siècle* decor. It's very popular. Prices can be high except for the good value *menu*. Often very busy, so book ahead. Try the *terrine Ferranti,* the *feuilleté de langoustines,* and the delicious desserts. Owners Pierre Ferranti and Jean-Marie Bracco will make sure you have a magnificent evening. Closed Saturday lunch and Sunday.

Paul, 15 place Dauphine (tel. 43-54-21-48). Lovers of authentic Parisian bistros—and they don't come much more authentic than this—rejoice at the survival of Chez Paul. It's on the Ile de la Cité, between the Pont Neuf and the Palais de Justice, in one of the prettiest squares in Paris. Dining on the terrace is an experience to remember. The food is traditional: snails and calf's head in shallot sauce are long-time favorites. Closed Monday, Tuesday and August.

Pharamond, 24 rue de la Grande Truanderie (tel. 42-33-06-72). In the heart of Les Halles, with beautiful and original turn-of-the-century decor. Specializes in dishes from Normandy. Closed Sunday, Monday and July.

Rôtisserie-Rivoli, Hotel Inter-Continental, 3 rue de Castiglione (tel. 42-60-37-80). Although part of a luxury hotel, the Rôtisserie-Rivoli offers excellent value for money. Try the *menu:* it has two *plats du jour.* Chef Jean-Jacques Barbier makes a point of insisting on high quality and copious portions. There's an Italian-style patio for outdoor dining in the summer.

Le Tour de Montlhéry, 5 rue des Prouvaires (tel. 42-36-21-82). Better known as **Chez Denise,** you'll discover one of the few remaining Les Halles bistros here. The place hasn't changed in years and neither has the owner, Denise. Her food is hearty, simple and unvaryingly good, and the atmosphere is noisy and smoky. Open 24 hours a day; closed Saturday, Sunday and mid-July to mid-August.

Willi's Wine Bar, 13 rue des Petits Champs (tel. 42-61-05-09). A little bit of England flavored with Parisian panache. Impeccably-mannered young ladies of the very best breeding serve you good quality Anglo-French food, and wine by the glass. It's always crowded. Open from 11 A.M. to 11 P.M. Closed Sundays and public holidays.

SECOND ARRONDISSEMENT

L'Amanguier, 110 rue de Richelieu (tel. 42-96-37-79). Like a summer's day in the country. The captivating green-and-white decor, with comfortable leather-and-cane upholstery, and the short but imaginative menu, with extremely reasonable prices, make this a real find. The desserts are particularly good. Near the Bourse and quite close to the Opéra. Open to midnight. Closed May 1.

Drouant, 16 rue Gaillon (tel. 42-65-15-16). This elegant restaurant and café is a Paris institution where France's highest literary prize, the Prix Goncourt, has been awarded since 1914. The glamorous café serves rather traditional, bourgeois cuisine, with an accent on seafood. The more sophisticated—and expensive—restaurant offers excellent *nouvelle* dishes. Try the warm oysters with caviar, the rabbit with fresh herbs, or the frog pastry with garlic cream. Closed weekends.

L'Escargot Montorgueil, 38 rue Montorgueil (tel. 42-36-83-51). Near what used to be Les Halles food market. Opened in the 1830s and still going strong, with delightful 19th-century decor of mirrors and traditional wall sofas. A chic clientele. Snails, of course, and many other good dishes. Closed Monday lunchtime, May 1 and one week around August 15.

Le Petit Coin de la Bourse, 16 rue Feydeau (tel. 45-08-00-08). Another businessman's restaurant, with mouthwatering food at excellent prices. Lunch reservations essential. Try *Symphonie de poisson marinés* or *Saumon sauvage à l'oseille.* And don't miss the exquisite *Tarte aux pommes:* it's always made specially, so you have to order it more or less as you arrive. Closed weekends.

Pierre à la Fontaine Gaillon, pl. Gaillon (tel. 42-65-87-04). A delightful restaurant, with excellent and friendly service. There's a leafy enclosed terrace in the summer. The food is traditional for the most part, and first class. This is another good place to come after the opera. Closed August, Saturday for lunch, and Sunday.

Pile ou Face, 52bis rue Notre Dame des Victoires (tel. 42-33-64-33). Tiny upstairs diningroom, popular at lunchtime with stockbrokers from the nearby Bourse, and with couples seeking romance in the evening. *Grande cuisine* with a sophisticated twist. Prices are moderate. Closed weekends, August, and last week in December.

THIRD ARRONDISSEMENT

L'Alisier, 26 rue de Montmorency (tel. 42-72-31-04). A little gem of a bistro in the heart of the Marais. Good fish, a *foie gras de canard* that's absolutely out of this world, and sea bass terrine with sea urchin sauce. Closed Saturday lunch and Sunday.

L'Ambassade d'Auvergne, 22 rue du Grenier-St.-Lazare (tel. 42-72-31-22). Just behind Beaubourg, this hearty regional restaurant is run by the Petrucci family. Among the treats offered here are *Mourtayrol,* a *pot-au-feu* from the Auvergne the likes of which you will never have tasted before; *Estofinado,* a mouth-watering fish dish; and a sensational tripe, spinach, and apple concoction that answers to the name of *Tripous à l'Estragon pommes fondantes.* Prices are high, but well worth it. Closed Sunday.

L'Ami Louis, 32 rue de Vertbois (tel. 48-87-77-48). This is perhaps the ultimate Parisian bistro, though distinctly more expensive than most, and deservedly popular (book well in advance). The death in 1987 of longtime chef and owner Antoine Magnim seems to have been weathered successfully, and l'Ami shows every sign of continuing its time-honored traditions for many years yet. The cuisine is based predominantly on southwestern specialties. Try the lamb in spring, the foie gras and the steak pâté. Closed Monday, Tuesday, and July and August.

FOURTH ARRONDISSEMENT

La Colombe, 4 rue de la Colombe (tel. 46-33-37-08). This is in an exquisite 13th-century house on the quayside opposite Notre Dame. The patronne, Renata, rules this charming roost—the restaurant is home to 14 white doves—with its fresh new decor and covered terrace, while chef Eric has added a personal touch to the sophisticated, but traditional, French cuisine. There's an excellent Moderately priced menu served at lunchtime and until 9 P.M., and some delicious desserts. Closed Sunday, and Monday lunch.

Courrier Sud, 19 rue Francois-Miron (tel. 42-78-64-54). Spruce and rather discreet little bistro in the Marais that's ideal for *liaisons dangereuses* (though of course you don't *have* to be having an affair to come here). The food's simple, and excellently cooked in the traditional bistrot style. Prices are low for what's offered. Open late; closed lunchtime and Sunday.

Le Domarais, 53bis rue des Francs-Bourgeois (tel. 42-74-54-17). From the outside this place looks as though it's part of the Banque Crédit Municipal de Commerce. But head through the courtyard and you step into a richly luxurious salon, with glass dome, deeply-lacquered wood, gold leaf, plants, and classical statues. The food is every bit as good as the astounding decor, with an equal mixture of *nouvelle* and *bourgeois cuisine.* Excellent wines. Closed weekends, August, and Christmas.

Guirlande de Julie, 25 place des Vosges (tel. 48-87-94-07). The combination of a location on the classy place des Vosges and simple specialties from southwestern France—try the duck or the perennially popular *pot au feu*—has made this restaurant a firm favorite. You can eat in one of two contrasting rooms: one in red brick, reflecting the square outside; the other fresh and summery. In summer, try for a table on a leafy terrace. Remember your jacket and tie. Closed Monday, Tuesday and December 20 to January 20.

Quai des Ormes, 72 quai de l'Hôtel de Ville (tel. 42-74-72-22). A rather chic restaurant, very well located by the Seine. Serves *nouvelle cuisine,* and has good value *menus* for lunch. Closed weekends and August.

FIFTH ARRONDISSEMENT

Atelier Maître Albert, 1 rue Maître Albert (tel. 46-33-13-78). This is seriously solid food, with the added benefit of a roaring log fire in the winter and air-conditioning in the summer. The menu's simple, but ultra-reliable. Open late. Closed weekends and public holidays.

Le Balzar, 49 rue des Ecoles (tel. 43-54-13-67). A genuine *brasserie,* complete with waiters in long white aprons and worthily traditional food. Low prices and terrific atmosphere. *Very* busy at lunch. Closed August.

Dodin Bouffant, 25 rue Frédéric-Sauton (tel. 43-25-25-14). Maurice and Danielle Cartier have been running this lively, upmarket brasserie for years, and have built up a large clientele of "regulars" who never tire of the delicious seafood and fish. Great salt-water tanks wait in the cellars below, alive with oysters, lobsters, and fish of every description. Exquisite desserts, wines fit for a king, outdoor dining, and remarkably reasonable prices complete the picture, but reserve well ahead. Closed Sunday.

Perraudin, 157 rue St. Jacques (tel. 46-33-15-75). Classical small bistro near the Sorbonne and the Panthéon; a rendezvous for poets, students, and professors. Traditional French cooking and atmosphere. Very reasonable *menus,* with specialties including *boeuf bourguignon à l'ancienne,* onion soup, *gratin dauphinois,* and a French Sunday brunch. On the corner of rue St. Jacques and rue Soufflot.

La Tour d'Argent, 15 quai de la Tournelle (tel. 43-54-23-31). This is probably the most expensive restaurant in Paris. Certainly it's the most famous. You pay for a table overlooking Notre Dame (illuminated at night), perfect service that ministers to your every whim, and the highest of *haute cuisine.* The food—known more for its finesse than its panache, with duck cooked in its own blood a classic—has maintained its high standards under new chef Manuel Martinez. There's a fixed priced *menu* at lunch that works out at about half the price of eating *à la carte.* There's just one snag, however. It's almost impossible to get in. Reserve days, weeks, months ahead. Closed Monday.

SIXTH ARRONDISSEMENT

Aux Charpentiers, 10 rue Mabillon (tel. 43-26-30-05). Classic Parisian bistro, unpretentious and altogether delightful. Used to be the headquarters of the Carpenters' Guild. Plain, straightforward, homey dishes, that are very reasonably priced. Closed Sunday, and New Year.

Chez Papa, 3 rue St. Benoît (tel. 42-86-99-63). The refreshing open-plan decor makes a pleasant change from the bustle and tightly packed tables of most St.-Germain restaurants. A shiny black, baby grand piano, surrounded by a host of house plants, stands out against the white of the walls and high ceiling. There's soft music from 9 every evening. The cuisine is also surprisingly light considering that the dishes are more usually associated with the sturdiest of French traditions—snails, *cassoulet, pot au feu.* Brunch on Sunday and a good lunchtime *menu* make Chez Papa an ideal lunch or dinner spot. Open year-round, except Monday lunch.

Closerie des Lilas, 171 blvd. du Montparnasse (tel. 43-26-70-50). On the corner of the blvd. St.-Michel and the blvd. du Montparnasse, the Closerie des Lilas has been an essential part of the Left Bank scene since it opened in 1907. Hemingway was here so regularly that a plaque commemorates his favorite spot at the bar. Though the lilacs have disappeared from the terrace, the place is as popular as it was in its heyday in the 1930s. Straightforward traditional fare is the order of the day: try the oysters. The adjoining brasserie offers much the same food at lower prices. Open year-round until 1 A.M.

La Méditerrannée, 2 place de l'Odéon (tel. 43-26-36-72). This is one of the city's oldest and most popular fish restaurants, still largely unchanged from the days when Jean Cocteau and Orson Welles were regulars, despite a certain amount of sprucing up in 1987. The terrace overlooks the relatively quiet place de l'Odéon and Odéon theater, making outdoor dining here a surprisingly soothing—if rather expensive—experience in this otherwise busy part of town. Open daily year-round until midnight.

La Petite Cour, 10 rue Mabillon (tel. 45-26-52-26). As the name implies, you can dine in the courtyard in summer, but there's a cozy atmosphere inside. The cuisine is mainly *nouvelle,* with an accent on herbs and spices and good, fresh ingredients. Try the fillet of turbot with green cabbage or scallops with horseradish and fresh pasta. There's a range of good set menus. Closed Sunday, and Monday lunch.

Petit St.-Benoît, 4 rue St-Benoît (tel. 42-60-27-92). This is a wonderful place. Small, inexpensive, always crowded, very simple—the true heart of St.-Germain beats inside its plain walls. Likely as not you'll find yourself sharing a table, but you can be sure it'll be with a kindred spirit. Closed weekends.

Le Petit Zinc, 25 rue de Buci (tel. 46-33-51-66). An old favorite—ever popular, ever crowded, with tables outside in summer. In common with many Parisian restaurants, it serves excellent oysters. Open till 3 A.M.

Le Procope, 13 rue de l'Ancienne Comédie (tel. 43-26-99-20). Founded in 1686 by an Italian, Francesco Procopio, this is said to be the oldest café in Paris and was long famous as a literary meeting place. Voltaire, Balzac and Victor Hugo were all regulars. The Blanc brothers, who already owned several other popular Parisian brasseries, including Au Pied du Cochon in Les Halles, took it over in 1987 and have given the old place a facelift, but they haven't changed the style of the good, solid, bourgeois cuisine. Open year-round till 2 A.M.

SEVENTH ARRONDISSEMENT

Chez des Anges, 54 blvd. de Latour-Maubourg (tel. 47-53-84-99). A spacious and comfortable spot near Les Invalides, offering a judicious mixture of *nouvelle* and classical cooking, the latter mostly from Burgundy. Expensive, but generally good to know. Closed Sunday for dinner.

La Ferme St. Simon, 6 rue St. Simon (tel. 45-48-35-74). Run by a leading French television personality and her husband, La Ferme St. Simon is a lively, very Parisian gastronomic highspot, especially popular with politicians from the nearby National Assembly. The food is an imaginative combination of classic and *nouvelle.* Among the specialties are ray fish steamed with tomatoes and spices, and veal *blanquette a l'ancienne.* Closed Saturday lunch, Sunday and August.

La Fontaine de Mars, 129 rue St.-Dominique (tel. 47-05-46-44). Typically French little restaurant near the Eiffel Tower. It's very much a no-frills place, but its straightforward home cooking has long been popular with the locals in this chic area. You can eat outside in the summer by a fountain in the little square. Prices are definitely low for what's offered. Closed Saturday for dinner, Sunday, and August.

Jules Verne, Entrance by Pilier Sud. Eiffel Tower (tel. 45-55-61-44). Opened only in 1985, this restaurant on the second story of the Eiffel Tower is very much more than just a gimmick. The setting is, of course, incomparable, but it's the food that rules supreme here. Prices are very high and reservations hard to come by, but if you can get in it's not an experience you'll forget quickly—this is really a view to dine by.

La Petite Chaise, 36 rue de Grenelle (tel. 42-22-13-35). One of the oldest restaurants in Paris, and still always full. Charming, slightly shabby and traditional atmosphere. The cooking is traditional, too, and excellent value. Open every day.

Au Quai d'Orsay, 49 quai d'Orsay (tel. 47-05-69-09). This pleasing spot has long been fashionable, and never seems to lose its popularity. Good value traditional dishes, very carefully cooked, with some highly imaginative touches; and all at moderate prices. Open daily year-round.

EIGHTH ARRONDISSEMENT

Alsace, 39 av. des Champs Elysées (tel. 43-59-44-24). Chic brasserie serving *choucroute,* beautifully fresh seafood, and superb fruit tarts, as well as the delicious light wines for which Alsace is famous. Has a shop selling regional delicacies next door. Open all day and all night.

Lucas-Carton, 9 pl. de la Madeleine (tel. 42-65-22-90). The Lucas-Carton has long been famed for its magnificent Belle Epoque *art nouveau* decor. Now, however, it also boasts a resident genius in the kitchens, Alain Senderens, the master of *nouvelle cuisine* at its subtle best. This is a place for true aficionados. Very expensive. Closed weekends, most of August, and Christmas.

Maxim's, 3 rue Royale (tel. 42-65-27-94). Another Belle Epoque landmark. This ultra-chic restaurant is today a part of couturier Pierre Cardin's empire, under whose auspices it has been revitalized from top to toe. Prices are very high, but more moderate meals are served on the second floor, and there's also a fixed-priced after-theater supper served from 11 P.M. Open to 1 A.M., closed Sunday.

Taillevent, 15 rue Lamennais (tel. 45-63-39-94). If you reserve several months in advance for dinner, and several weeks in advance for lunch, there's a fighting chance you might get a table here. Is this the best restaurant in Paris? Probably, but who can say for sure? Superb *nouvelle cuisine,* perfect service, exquisite surroundings, a truly phenomenal wine list. Closed weekends, one week in February and August, and public holidays.

NINTH ARRONDISSEMENT

Chartier, 7 rue du Faubourg Montmartre (tel. 47-70-86-29). Chartier's low prices, spacious turn-of-the-century decor, hectic atmosphere and classic fare have earned it an enviable reputation as one of the best-value places to eat in Paris. The choice isn't wide, but the food is always hearty and filling. Try the steak tartare if it's on the menu, and snails if you're feeling adventurous. You can't book so get there early or expect to wait. Open daily year-round.

ELEVENTH ARRONDISSEMENT

Chez Philippe (Auberge Pyrénées-Cévennes), 106 rue de la Folie-Méricourt (tel. 43-57-33-78). Old café with exquisite food from the southwest of France. Last orders at 10:30 P.M. Closed Saturday, Sunday, and August.

FIFTEENTH ARRONDISSEMENT

La Maison Blanche, 82 blvd. Lefebvre (tel. 48-28-38-83). A fashionable restaurant in an otherwise unfashionable district. Bouquets of flowers everywhere enhance the elegant decor. The modern-style cuisine has a very personal touch with enticing specialties like codfish in spices. Some of the best-value eating in Paris. Closed Saturday for lunch, all day Sunday, Monday, and two weeks in September.

SEVENTEENTH ARRONDISSEMENT

La Toque, 16 rue de Tocqueville (tel. 42-27-97-75). Tiny but comfortable bistro serving excellent food (chef Jacky Joubert worked with Michel Guérard). Good value *menu.* Closed Saturday, Sunday, August, and Christmas.

Cafés and Bars

Cafés are a central part of the Parisian scene, both by day and by night. People-watching from a sidewalk café is one of the eternal delights of this city, one that's hard to tire of. There are hundreds—maybe thousands—of cafés all over Paris, ranging from the chic spots on the Champs Elysées and the intellectual haunts in Saint-Germain and Montparnasse to the simple neighborhood corner cafés where the locals gather to gossip and have a bite to eat.

Prices vary greatly. The smart places can be surprisingly expensive. Elsewhere, prices are generally very low. But you can linger for as long as you want over your coffee or drink, so even the most expensive places won't break the bank. Prices are naturally lower if you stand at the bar rather than have a waiter or waitress serve you at a table. But don't order from the bar and then move to a table. The manager will certainly come over and rebuke you.

Café de la Paix, 5 pl. de l'Opéra, 9e. Just by the Opéra and long popular with wealthy foreign tourists. Try also the restaurant here, the *Opéra*.

La Coupole, 102 blvd. du Montparnasse, 14e. The **Flo** group—owners of a handful of prestigious Parisian brasseries—bought this famous Left Bank haunt last year and have given it a facelift, but it's kept its former atmosphere. Times have changed, of course, since the days when Joyce, Hemingway, Pound, Cocteau, et al, used to come here, but this substantial café-brasserie is still well worth a visit.

Deux Magots, 6 place St.-Germain-des-Prés, 6e. Not the intellectuals' mecca it was in the heyday of existentialism when Sartre and Co. virtually lived here, but still fashionable, and probably the best place for people-watching. You even get street entertainment thrown in every once in a while: fire-eaters, acrobats, mimes, and the like.

Le Dôme, 108 blvd. du Montparnasse, 14e. This is the other great Montparnasse café. The new decor—a peculiar species of fake *art nouveau*—is not entirely successful, but for a taste of café-society Le Dôme is still one of *the* places to head for.

Le Flore, 172 blvd. St.-Germain, 6e. Next door to the Deux Magots, though it doesn't share its unbeatable corner location. Upstairs is a traditional gay meeting place, but the sidewalk tables are for all comers. It changed hands a few years back, but the new owners have had to guarantee to leave it just as it's always been.

Fouquet's, 99 av. des Champs-Elysées, 8e. Very chic and predictably expensive. This is a place to be seen. There's a good bar, too. Open 8 A.M. till 2 the following morning.

Lipp, 151 blvd. St.-Germain, 6e. Officially a brasserie—and as such it's a regular institution, and favorite haunt of politicos, writers, and film folk—this is still a good place to come for just a coffee or aperitif.

Le Sélect, 99 blvd. du Montparnasse, 6e. Much of the atmosphere of old Montparnasse lingers on here, despite the rebuilding that has done so much to transform the area. Open late.

BARS

With cafés so ubiquitous, Paris has few regular bars. After all, if you can always get a drink in a café, who needs a bar? But there's a fair sprinkling nonetheless (many confusingly called cafés). Among the more popular are:

Le Bar, 38 rue de Condé, 6e. There's no problem trying to figure out if this place is a bar or a café. This is one of the classic spots, and enduringly popular. It's always had a sophisticated clientele, especially from 2 in the morning, when it's just beginning to hit its stride.

Les Bouchons, 19 rue des Halles, 1er. Piano bar with entertainment from 11 P.M. until 2 A.M. Try the first-floor restaurant.

Le Calvados, 40 av. Pierre-Ier-de-Serbie, 8e. A favorite haunt of the smart drinking set. This, too, is very much an after-hours bar; not surprisingly, seeing as it's open 24 hours a day.

City Rock Café, 72 av. des Champs-Elysées, 8e. Open till 4 A.M., this place is the half-brother of the Hard Rock in London and New York. It's all here . . . a Cadillac that belonged to Elvis, a dress that belonged to Marilyn Monroe, one of Indiana Jones' shirts. There are regular gigs, too; past stars have included Michel Axel, Duran Duran, and Ringo. Hamburgers and banana splits are very much the order of the day.

La Closerie des Lilas, 171 blvd. du Montparnasse, 6e. Voices have been raised claiming that this firmly artistic and literary spot is overrated these days, a shadow of its former self. But it's still going strong, and very popular for a lateish drink. Prices are high though. Open 10:30 A.M.–2:20 A.M.

Harry's (New York) Bar, 5 rue Daunou, 2e. Opened originally in 1911, Harry's Bar has never looked back. The Hemingway era may be long gone now, but Harry's Bar goes on. It's always had an American slant, and it stays open year-round till 4 A.M.

Magnetic-Terrace, 12 rue de la Cossonnerie, 1er. This place could equally well qualify as a café, or even a restaurant. But, leaving aside the restaurant and the *salon du thé* on the second floor, the Californian video piano-bar on the first floor is what attracts most. Service in short shorts, an excellent pianist, and the Magnetic cocktails to pulverize you.

Rosebud, 11bis rue Delambre, 14e (tel. 43-35-38-54). A bit pseudo, but great after hours. Small, smoky and full of would-be Parisians, most of them over 40. Teenies give it a miss.

WINE BARS

As a general rule, the French eat their main meal at lunch. So it can be difficult to find a place for a light lunch if you're not in the mood for just a sandwich or other café food. But over the last few years it's become fashionable among the city's well-heeled younger set to go to wine bars for a glass of wine and a tasty light meal of pâté, cold cuts, or cheese.

Wine bars of this type are mushrooming throughout the city now, mostly full of Yuppies and other chic types, plus a sprinkling of old timers who've lived in the district for years. They should not, however, be confused with the old-style *bistrots à vin*. These are principally dives for hardened local drinkers, and rarely offer much in the way of food.

The new wine bars don't stay open late, however, so don't count on them for an evening meal. Few are open at weekends.

Blue Fox, 25 rue Royale, 8e. In the Cité Berryer. Run by Steven Spurrier, who also presides over the Moulin du Village and the Académie du Vin.

L'Ecluse, 15 quai des Grands-Augustins, 6e. Once a typical Left-Bank cabaret, today this is a slick wine bar with converted gas lamps, *art nouveau* posters, and a distinctly up-market clientele. It's been such a success that it's spawned a mini-chain all over the city, even in chic Neuilly. You'll find the others at: rue Mondétour, 1er; rue du Pont-de-Lodi, 6e; 15 pl. de la Madeleine, 8e; 64 rue du François-1er; 8e; 2 rue du Général Berticr, Ncuilly. All are open late.

Juveniles, 47 rue de Richelieu, 1er (tel. 42-97-46-49). This is a trendy new offshoot of Willi's Wine Bar, run by some charming young English ladies who serve top-rate wine and original but excellent food to help keep you sober. There's not much room so make sure you book. Open till late.

Le Petit Bacchus, 13 rue du Cherche-Midi, 6e. Wine to go as well as to drink here. Closes at 7:15 P.M.

La Tartine, 24 rue du Rivoli, 4e. Typical Parisian spot, with a regular clientele, a good range of wines, and some delicious tartines, the nearest the French get to bread and cheese.

It's French cheese, of course, or there's salami, or pâté. Friendly atmosphere. Open till around 10 P.M.

JUICE BARS

Juice bars are newcomers to Paris. They're rapidly catching on among the younger generation, who more alert to health-food fads than their elders. The majority of these pleasantly casual places are near the place St.-Michel, with several of them right by the Seine. They're good for a quick break between sightseeing visits, and many also serve good homemade ice cream and milkshakes.

Le Paradis du Fruit, 28 rue Louis-le-Grand 2e; and 29 quai des Grands-Augustins, 6e. Salads and tasty pâtisseries. Both open till 2 A.M.

La Passion du Fruit, 71 quai de la Tournelle, 5e. Opposite the Ile St.-Louis and handy for Notre Dame. Open till 2 A.M., but closed afternoons.

Nightlife

Paris has successfully sustained its reputation as one of the great nightlife capitals of the world. And of no area of the multi-faceted world of nightlife is this more true than the great revues and shows. Images of the Can-Can, the Folies-Bergère, the Moulin Rouge, Mistinguett, Maurice Chevalier, Josephine Baker, and the Bluebell Girls have proved amazingly durable. And indeed a great many of the larger shows are extremely good: professional, lavish, slick, and spectacular. But they're not inexpensive, and you'll find you're "expected" to drink champagne. Still, they're packing 'em in night after night, so reserve several days ahead if you want to be sure of getting a decent table. But don't be disappointed if your fellow guests are all tourists. The Japanese in particular have a weakness for Parisian nightlife.

All the revues feature seminude bodies as shiny and innocuous as Playboy centerfolds. If your tastes run to something a little rawer, head for the rue St.-Denis, the traditional red-light district. But avoid Pigalle, up by Montmartre. It's as sordid as they come these days.

SHOWS

Alcazar de Paris, 62 rue Mazarine, 6e (tel. 43-29-02-20). Well-known spot in St.-Germain. Loud and bitchy transvestite revues are the specialty, so it helps if you know the odd French insult.

Don Camilo, 10 rue des Sts.-Pères, 7e (tel. 42-60-82-84). An old favorite. Elegant and sophisticated cabaret show, and excellent food. Prices are more reasonable than most.

Le Caveau des Oubliettes, 52 rue Galande, 5e (tel. 43-54-94-97). This famous medieval cellar, complete with fake decor and costumed waiters, seems to have been going for ever. But for nostalgia and kitsch it's unbeatable. Lots of Piaf.

Crazy Horse Saloon, 12 av. George-V, 8e (tel. 47-23-32-32). This claims to be the world's top nude show. If popularity is anything to go by, it's hard to disagree. The theater was extensively modernized in 1988 and offers cheap(ish) standing-room tickets (190 frs.) that include the price of one drink. Shows nightly at 9 and 11:30; three shows on Saturday at 8, 10, and 12:50.

Chez Félix, 23 rue Mouffetard, 5e (tel. 47-07-68-78). Located in the picturesque Contrescarpe area. Have just a drink, or go the whole hog and have a candle-lit dinner. There's live Brazilian music and dancing in the atmospheric cellars, and a floor show upstairs. Atmospheric and light-hearted. Closed on Sunday and Monday.

Folies-Bergère, 32 rue Richer, 9e (tel. 42-46-77-11). Strictly a theater, where your ticket buys you a seat for the show rather than dinner or a drink. It's still probably the best-known name, with extravagant sets, showy costumes, elaborate sound effects, and spectacular semi-nude dancers, but the glorious days of Chevalier and Mistinguett have long since faded. Still, a certain glamor lingers on.

Le Lapin Agile, 22 rue des Saules, 18e (tel. 46-06-85-87). Le Lapin Agile won its reputation in the early years of the century when Montmartre's artist colony caroused their nights away here. But it's still fun, even if strictly run for the benefit of tourists now. The wooden tables, lively atmosphere, and the show—mostly old French songs, with a handful of newer ones—remain a winning combination.

Lido, 116bis av. des Champs-Elysées, 8e (tel. 45-63-11-61). This is *the* place for spectacular entertainment on the grand scale. Dazzling technical trickery, enormous sets, phenomenal costumes, computerized choreography, and the Bluebell Girls add up to the most lavish show of its kind in Paris. The food is adequate, or worse, but the show's the thing. Dinner-dance at 8, shows at 10:15 and 12:30.

Michou, 80 rue des Martyrs, 18e (tel. 46–06–16–04). Great show, with dinner, every evening. You must book well in advance. Close to Montmartre.

Milliardaire, 68 rue Pierre-Charron, 8e (tel. 42-25-25-17). Once you've been to the Crazy Horse, this is the place to come to see a classy strip (Le Milliardaire used to be known as Le Sexy, and for good reasons). Not much has changed. There's a special late show at 2:30 A.M.

Moulin Rouge, pl. Blanche, 19e (tel. 46-06-00-19). Still cashing in on the most famous name from Montmartre's heyday, and still specializing in the one and only Can-Can. It's owned and run by the same people as the Lido, so it's very professional if slightly less expensive than its stable-mate. Dinner-dance at 8, shows at 10 and 12.

Le Paradis Latin, 28 rue du Cardinal-Lemoine, 5e (tel. 43-29-07-07). Lively and crowded, with amazing architecture. The shows regularly attract big names, but are otherwise a bit faded at the edges now. Dinner and show at 8, and "champagne revue" at 10. Closed Tuesday.

CLUBS

Private clubs in Paris are both extremely expensive—a bottle of whiskey has been known to sell for 1,000 frs.—and notoriously difficult to get into. "Club" is a misnomer really, though. Calling a place a club is principally just an excuse to keep out anyone whose face doesn't fit. The best *entrée* is, inevitably, knowing the right people. Failing that, do what you can to look interesting, desirable, chic, and glamorous. And if you still can't get in, never mind. Paris has a great deal more to offer.

L'Apocalypse, 40 rue du Colisée, 8e (tel. 42-25-11-68). Very expensive, very exclusive, and much loved by the super-rich-playboy-beautiful-people-celebrity set.

Cabaret 78, 78 ave. des Champs-Elysées, 8e (tel. 43-59-09-99). It may not be as trendy as it was, but the trapeze artists, the underground pool, the light shows, and stock-exchange reports are all still very much in evidence.

Princesse, 15 rue Princesse, 6e (tel. 43-26-90-22). If you can get into this place it's a real experience. Members only, but if you happen to be Bianca Jagger there's a chance they might let you in on a quiet night. The prettiest women, the smartest names—you name it, they're all here. Excellent bar and restaurant, good music, videos, discos, the lot.

Régine's, 49 rue Ponthieu, 8e (tel. 43-59-21-60). Régine's may be a teeny bit passé now, but it's still pretty luxurious and chic. Excellent food, and jet-setters of all types.

DISCOS

Paris is packed with discos of every description these days. Some are stylish, some are merely tawdry. Most are in between. Unfortunately, keeping track of them is next to impossible. New ones open and close seemingly overnight. Others change their names every few months, though their decor and ambience frequently weather the changes. Those listed here have proved fairly durable, but don't be surprised if they've changed names, moved premises, folded, or disappeared from the face of the earth by the time you read this.

Most open around 10 or 10:30 and stay on the boil till dawn. Some are closed on Mondays, but a fair number are also open on Sunday afternoons. A few will let in girls free during the week or at other quiet spells.

Les Bains, 7 rue du Bourg-l'Abbé, 3e (tel. 48-87-01-80). Originally a public bath house, this subsequently became a serious haunt for New Wave devotees. Today, with a swimming pool much in evidence, and after a great deal of renovation, it's among the city's most popular spots. Very trendy.

Balajo, 9 rue de Lappe, 11e (tel. 47-00-07-87). This is one of the best nightspots in Paris. The decor hasn't changed for years and has something delightfully corny about it, but the atmosphere—after 10:30 or 11—is hectic, amusing, and not to be taken too seriously. That said, dancing is a serious affair here. This is no boring disco joint: the music changes every night. There's rock, Tamla Motown, old fashioned French accordion music and the inevitable disco. Check out what it is before you turn up. Closed Tuesday.

Club Zed, 2 rue des Anglais, 5e (tel. 43-54-93-78). Rock'n'roll is the staple diet here, with jazz and java on Thursday. Closed Sunday–Tuesday.

Le Gibus, 18 rue fbg. du Temple, 10e (tel. 47-00-78-88). Here today and gone tomorrow. It's very "in" at the moment, but may be empty in a few months. There's a distinctly cosmopolitan feel. Anything goes.

La Main Jaune, rue du Caporal-Peugeot, 17e (tel. 47-63-26-47). A good place to meet the young Parisians, and to dance on roller skates.

Music, Movies, and Theaters

For details on how to find out what's playing in Paris, see "What's On" in *Paris Briefing*.

MUSIC

JAZZ. The French take jazz seriously and Paris is one of the great jazz cities of the world, with several specialist record shops and an array of clubs. Every type of jazz is available, from the stolidly traditional through classic bebop to jazz-rock and, increasingly, South American and African off-shoots.

For precise details of who's on when, see either of the excellent specialist magazines, *Jazz Hot* or *Jazz Magazine,* and listen to the jazz programs on France Musique. Remember that nothing gets going until 10 or 11 P.M., credit cards are almost never accepted, and, although prices are generally reasonable, they vary according to the attraction.

Le Caméléon, 6 rue Chevreuse, 6e (tel. 43-20-63-43). There was a time when you could be sure of an enthusiastic crowd in this dark record bar, with its downstairs cellar for live music and dancing. It's quieter these days, though the choice of records is still discriminating. Decent range of beers and whiskies, but no exotic cocktails. Inexpensive.

Le Caveau de la Huchette, 5 rue de la Huchette, 5e (tel. 43-26-65-05). Large stone cellar in student (and tourist) quarter. An illustrious history, but today the place is a little past its prime. It mainly features traditional French bands. Good for dancing and, if you're young, making contact. Stays open especially late on Fridays and Saturdays. Entrance 45 frs. Inexpensive drinks.

Le Montana, 28 rue St.-Benoît, 6e (tel. 45-48-93-08). An informal bar in the heart of Saint-Germain-des-Prés. It has some excellent live jazz bands and is reasonably priced.

New Morning, 7–9 rue des Petites Ecuries, 10e (tel. 45-23-51-41). A large room (seats over 400) with excellent sound and visibility. Although it's only been going since 1981, this is now the best club in Paris, if not in Europe, and the premier venue for visiting American musicians, top French groups, and fashionable *salsa* bands. A serious place, for aficionados only. Entrance prices range from 90–120 frs. Moderate range of cocktails, spirits, and beers.

Le Petit Journal, 71 blvd. St.-Michel, 5e (tel. 43-26-28-59). Well run and long established club, opposite the Luxembourg Gardens, specializing in live traditional and mainstream jazz. Individual booths, unusual cocktails, lavish salads and icecreams. Entrance and first drink 80 frs. Closed Sunday and August.

Le Petit Opportun, 15 rue des Lavandières-Sainte-Opportune, 1e (tel. 42-36-01-36). Converted bistro with cramped atmospheric basement (seats 50) often featuring topflight American soloists with French rhythm sections. Entrance and first drink up to 100 frs. At street level there's a pleasant bar with recorded music and less expensive drinks.

Slow Club, 130 rue de Rivoli, 1e (tel. 42-33-84-30). Longestablished dancing club often presenting Maxim Saury's well-known traditional band. Open especially late at weekends. Entrance 50–62 frs.; inexpensive drinks.

Le Sunset, 60 rue des Lombards, 1e (tel. 40-26-46-60). In the reinvigorated Les Halles area: a small whitewashed cellar with first-rate live music. Clientele is young, chic, and there to listen. Open very late, and stays crowded. Entrance, including first drink, about 80 frs., second drink 50 frs. Long list of cocktails.

ROCK. Unlike French jazz, French rock is generally not considered to be up to much. It has certainly never achieved an international reputation. You should be able to get to hear live rock music in the following places, most of which charge in the region of 80–100 frs. entrance money, including the first drink, and around 45–55 frs. for subsequent drinks. Prices often rise on weekends, when most places get pretty crowded. Most don't get going properly till 11:30 or midnight, and stay open through to dawn or thereabouts.

Les Bains, 7 rue du Bourg-l'Abbé, 3 (tel. 48-87-01-80). See "Discos" in *Nightlife* chapter. Has live rock on Wednesday nights.

Balajo, 9 rue de Lappe, 11e (tel. 47-00-07-87). This is one of the best disco-cum-nightclubs in Paris. The music changes nightly so if you're a rock fan try and make it on a Monday. See "Discos" in *Nightlife* chapter.

Bus Palladium, 6 rue Fontaine, 9e (tel. 48-74-54-99). On the edge of Montmartre, youthful clientele, mostly live rock, some discs.

Club Zed, 2 rue des Anglais, 5e (tel. 43-54-93-78). See "Discos" in *Nightlife* chapter. Has live rock at times.

Gibus, 18 rue fbg. du Temple, 10e (tel. 47-00-78-80). See "Discos" in *Nightlife* chapter. Currently *the* place for rock.

CLASSICAL CONCERTS. Paris is one of Europe's liveliest cities for contemporary music these days. This is thanks partly to the influence of Pierre Boulez, France's greatest living composer-conductor, who heads the contemporary music section at the **Pompidou/Beaubourg Center.** Interesting concerts are given there most of the year. Classical concerts are often held in the city's concert halls and, perhaps more interestingly for foreign visitors, in her historic churches. This is a splendid way of combining the delights of sightseeing with listening to music. Have a look to see if there's a concert being performed in **Notre-Dame, Saint-Louis-des-Invalides, Saint-Germain-l'Auxerrois, Saint-Merri, Saint-Etienne du Mont,**

Saint-Louis-en-l'Ile or the **Sainte Chapelle,** all of which provide stunning settings. The concerts in the marvelous Gothic Sainte Chapelle are out of this world, especially if you're lucky enough to hit a time when they're performed by candlelight. Leaflets covering six months of programs can be obtained from the Paris Tourist Office or the Sainte Chapelle itself, and you'd be well advised to reserve well ahead if possible.

In the summer, the excellent *Festival de l'Ile-de-France* stages fine concerts of classical music in churches, abbeys, châteaux, and town halls all over the Ile de France, the area immediately around Paris. This again gives you an opportunity to combine an evening's concert-going with a spot of sightseeing. And during the *Festival du Marais* in Paris, concerts are often performed in the courtyards of the Marais's beautifully restored mansions.

MOVIES

Paris has hundreds of movie houses, some huge and palatial, some tiny and uncomfortable. Parisians are far more addicted to the cinema as an art form than Londoners or New Yorkers, and you'll find that the latest films, French or foreign, are widely discussed. The letters "v.f." (*version française*) beside a foreign film in a newspaper or magazine listing mean that the movie has been dubbed into French; the letters "v.o." (*version originale*) mean that the movie is playing in the original language with French subtitles.

The bigger and more expensive movie houses are mostly on the Champs Elysées or around the Opéra. The smaller art houses are in the Latin Quarter or Saint-Germain-des-Prés. Programs change on Wednesdays. The standard program has movies showing at two-hourly intervals between around 2 P.M. and 10 P.M. (midnight on Saturday). Prices are lower on Mondays except when it is a public holiday.

Paris has two *cinémathèques,* showing classics from all over the world, one in the Beaubourg/Pompidou Center, 4e, the other at the Palais de Chaillot in the Place du Trocadéro, 16e.

THEATERS

NATIONAL THEATERS. The shows are naturally in French, so if your command of the language isn't great, you may find them heavy going. Paris's best-known "national" (i.e. state-subsidized) theaters are:

The **Comédie Française,** near the Opéra and beside the Palais-Royal in the place André-Malraux. The company specializes in performances of the great dramatists of the 17th century—Corneille, Molière, and Racine—but also ranges well beyond the classical repertoire, staging plays by modern playwrights from France and all over the world. Seats can be reserved in person a maximum of two weeks in advance.

The **Théâtre de Chaillot,** in the place du Trocadéro, has some interesting experimental shows from time to time.

The **Odéon,** in the place de l'Odéon in the Latin Quarter, is used mainly as an overspill for the Comédie Française, but also houses visiting companies, including major foreign troupes (such as Britain's Royal Shakespeare Company) playing in their own language.

The **Théâtre de la Ville** in the place du Châtelet stages a major international theater festival, plus opera and ballet at times.

COMMERCIAL THEATERS. For the many commercial theaters, most of which are in the Opéra area, you'll need to study lists of what's currently on. A surprising number of plays turn out to be translations of American or British hits, but you may find productions of movies by such well-known French dramatists as Jean Anouilh, Henri de Montherlant, or the Romanian-born Ionesco. Many English-speaking visitors find French acting rather "theatrical."

EXPERIMENTAL THEATERS. You may well find that one of the experimental theaters is more to your taste. True theater buffs should check out what's showing at the following:

Cartoucherie, av. de la Pyramide, on the edge of Paris at Vincennes. Several resident companies here, with invariably interesting, sometimes way-out, shows. At our presstime these four separate mini-theaters were operating, but be sure to check the latest position: **Epée de Bois,** tel. 48-08-39-74; **Théâtre de la Tempête,** tel. 43-28-36-36; **Atelier du Chaudron,** tel. 43-28-97-04; **Théâtre de l'Aquarium,** tel. 43-74-72-74.

Epicerie, 12 rue du Renard, 4e, tel. 42-72-23-41, near Beaubourg and the Hôtel de Ville.

Lucernaire, 53 rue Notre-Dame-des-Champs, 6e, tel. 45-44-57-34, with two separate theaters, the **Théâtre Noir** and the **Théâtre Rouge,** each generally offering two different shows nightly.

Renaud-Barrault, av. Franklin Roosevelt, 8e, tel. 42-56-70-80; the **Petite Salle** in this very attractive former ice-skating palace near the Rond-Point of the Champs-Elysées, now housing the world-famous Madeleine Renaud–Jean-Louis Barrault company, often has interesting semi-experimental shows. It's also a great place for lunch, far from the madding crowd.

OPERA AND BALLET

Fortunately, you don't need a knowledge of French to enjoy the excellent productions at the **Paris Opéra,** the opulent building in the place de l'Opéra, generally considered to be one of the world's great houses. But you'll probably have a lot of trouble getting tickets.

The **Opéra Comique** (also known as the **Salle Favart**) is Paris's second opera house. It specializes in opera with spoken dialogue (which is what the term *opéra comique* means).

The Opéra is also the home of the state-subsidized ballet company, which has a fairly high reputation. Much of the most interesting ballet in Paris comes during the annual November December Ballet Festival held in the recently restored, Art Deco-style **Théâtre des Champs-Elysées** in the avenue Montaigne. Major foreign companies and guest stars perform during this excellent festival. Other places where ballet is staged are the **Théâtre de la Ville,** at Châtelet, the huge **Palais des Congrès,** at Porte Maillot, and the **Palais des Sports** at the Porte de Versailles. This last is not as atmospheric as the Opéra, but it is able to seat thousands of people. The huge **Théâtre Musical de Paris,** also on place du Châtelet, offers opera and ballet intended for a more popular audience, with much lower seat prices than at the Opéra. You may also find productions at the ultra-modern **Palais Omni-sports de Bercy** in eastern Paris. The new **Opéra de la Bastille,** built to bring this "elitist" art form to a mass audience, was inaugurated in July 1989, but not scheduled to open to the public until spring 1990.

Keep an eye open for ballet performances during the *Festival du Marais* in the early summer, and the *Festival Estival* (Summer Festival), which runs from mid-July to around mid-September. Outside Paris, opera (and occasionally ballet) is staged in the pretty opera house in Versailles.

Shopping

We're ready to bet you'll find shopping in Paris one of the highlights of your trip. There's a huge range of shops, from the mammoth department stores to tiny back-street haunts selling a wide range of charming handmade gift items. And then there are the fabulous open-air markets, boasting everything from aardvarks to zebra fish.

Paris being a thoroughly cosmopolitan city, you can buy pretty much anything here. But so you can back home, too. So we've concentrated on the sorts of typically French goods you're likely to want to take back as souvenirs, or give to friends and family.

SHOPPING FACTS

Most shops are open from 9 or 10 A.M. to 6:30 or 7 P.M. Fashion boutiques and antique shops may not open until 10 and may shut for lunch, especially in the summer when some staff are on vacation. Small food shops open earlier (8 or 8:30) and don't close until around 7:30 or 8 P.M., but they have a long lunch break, usually from 1 to 3:30 or 4. Department stores stay open all day, from around 9:30 to 6:30, and often stay open late one night a week. Many small shops close for a month in the summer (usually August). when most of their regular customers are away from Paris, but a surprising number of shops are open on Sunday mornings, and small food shops are generally open in the morning on public holidays. However, Monday is a bad day for food shopping, as many food shops are closed in the morning. Many other shops that are open all day on Saturday may well close for at least part of Monday.

If you're resident outside France, you'll generally be able to take advantage of the tax-free refunds many stores offer. The best places to do so are the department stores and the larger fashion and perfume boutiques. A significant part of their business comes from tourists, and they have all the paperwork well organized. Other shops may do their best to be helpful, but the odds are they won't be equipped to deal efficiently with the formalities, and you may never get your refund. For details of how the scheme works, see "Tax Refunds" in *Paris Briefing*.

A good many larger stores will accept dollars or pounds—either travelers checks or bills—for goods. But their exchange rates often bear little more than a passing resemblance to the official one, and any gain in convenience may be paid for in hard cash, making this a mixed blessing. Credit cards are becoming more widely accepted, Visa and Eurocard/MasterCard especially.

You can have goods sent directly to your home, but this is a chancy business. Goods have often been "lost" en route. Many stores, even the largest, are ever more reluctant to do this now, fearing for their reputations. But if you do have goods sent home, expect them to take many weeks, even if they go by air.

DEPARTMENT STORES

The city has a large number of excellent department stores. **Au Printemps,** 64 blvd. Haussmann, 9e, claims to be the "most Parisian of the big stores." It is certainly one of the most upmarket, as is the long-famous **Galeries Lafayette,** next door at #40. These two huge stores have everything, including restaurants, hairdressers, and multilingual hostesses. Not far from here is the smaller; more select **Trois-Quartiers,** 17 blvd. de la Madeleine, 1er.

Two popular stores catering more to ordinary Parisians than to foreign tourists are close together in the Hôtel de Ville area: **La Samaritaine,** 19 rue de la Monnaie, 1er, with a roof terrace offering stunning views over the Seine; and the **Bazar de l'Hôtel de Ville,** 55 rue de le Verrerie, 4e (main entrances in the rue de Rivoli, just opposite the Hôtel de Ville), which is excellent for household articles.

The only department store on the Left Bank is **Au Bon Marché,** 38 rue de Sèvres, 7e, with a well-known antiques section, and a faithful following among local residents.

SHOPPING ARCADES AND MALLS

The city's covered shopping arcades, many dating from the 19th century, are peculiarly Parisian. The best have been splendidly restored to show off to full advantage their arching glass roofs, marble floors, brass lamps, and, in one or two instances, even an elaborate staircase.

Two of the most attractive are the **Galerie Véro-Dodat,** 19 rue Jean-Jacques Rousseau, 1er, with magnificent painted ceilings and slender copper pillars, and the **Galerie Vivienne,** 4 pl. des Petits-Champs, 3e, near the Bourse and the Bibliothèque Nationale, which has some particularly interesting shops, as well as a good tearoom. Other examples, all in the same central area of the Right Bank, are the **Passage des Pavillons,** 6 rue de Beaujolais, 1er; the **Passage des Princes,** 97 rue de Richelieu, 2e; and the **Passage des Panoramas,** 2e, the granddaddy of them all—it was opened to the public as long ago as 1800.

This 19th-century tradition has been revived in recent times with the building of several *galeries* off the Champs Elysées (all on the north side). The **Galerie du Claridge, Galeries Elysées 26, Galeries du Lido,** and **Galerie du Rond Point** are all worth seeking out. The **Forum des Halles** and the first floor of the **Tour Montparnasse** are larger versions still—more malls than arcades—though entirely lacking the architectural grace of the old arcades.

MARKETS

Paris's open-air **food markets** are an unending delight. The colorful pyramids of fruits and vegetables are particularly appealing, but don't touch the goods or you'll be treated to some equally colorful language from the stallholder!

Over Christmas and New Year the stallholders really go to town, vying with one another to produce the most tempting displays of seasonal specialties: fruits and nuts, every conceivable type of *charcuterie,* with *foie gras* and pâtés fashioned to look like miniature ducks, and terrines decorated with seasonal trimmings.

Every district has its own market, which may be held daily or just once or twice a week, though in all cases morning is always the best time to visit. Sunday is usually the best day for market lovers, and Monday the worst. The best-known of the food markets are: the centuries-old rue Mouffetard, 5e, in the heart of the Latin Quarter; the rue de Buci bang in the middle of St.-Germain-des-Prés; the rue Cler, 7e, near the Invalides and the Eiffel Tower; the rue Poncelet, 17e, close to pl. des Ternes; the rue Lepic, 18e, in Montmartre; and the pl. du Marché in Neuilly (just by the Les Sablons métro stop), this last a good bet if you feel like a Sunday stroll in the Bois de Boulogne (though it's also open Wednesday and Friday). The **Marché d'Aligre** (open Saturday, Sunday and Monday mornings, just beyond the Bastille in the 12th arondissement) is great fun. This is one of the poorer areas of Paris, so you won't see many tourists, but Parisians from all over the city know it and love it. Secondhand clothes sellers and *brocanteurs* (offering a mixture of junk and antiques) compete with the cries from fruit and vegetable stalls, bringing their prices down as the morning draws to a close. An Aligre highlight, especially on Sunday morning, is **Le Baron Rouge,** just off the market place. He will serve you a glass of wine of your choice while you listen to the latest addition to his jazz collection.

The most famous **flower market** is on the Ile de la Cité, near Notre Dame, but there are also good flower markets beside the church of La Madeleine, 8e, and in the pl. des Ternes, 17e. All are open daily except Monday from 8 to 7.

The most famous market of all is the Marché aux Puces, the **flea market,** founded in 1885. It's held around the Porte de St.-Ouen, 17e, and the Porte de Clignancourt, 18e, and spreads over an astounding six-and-a-half kilometers. It's open all day Saturday, Sunday, and Monday. The Puces is now more antique than bargain oriented and is no longer the cheap and cheerful place it once was—it's too commercial. But lunching on mussels and chips, a local specialty, adds to the local color.

PERFUMES

What could be more French than a bottle of one of the world's top perfumes? But buying perfumes here can be a complicated business, especially if you want the best possible price. Everybody seems to be offering discounts of one kind or another, and the hard sell is very much the norm. But if you're prepared to take your time and shop around, and take advantage of the tax refunds, there are some great bargains.

If you already know what you want, head for one of the upmarket discount stores. Try **Galerie Elysées 26** at 26 av. des Champs-Elysées, 8e; and 112 rue du fbg. St.-Honoré, 8e; or the old-established **Michel Swiss,** 16 rue de la Paix, 2e. **Paris Look,** 13 and 19 av. de l'Opéra, 1er, advertises 25% off the major names; and **Patchouli,** at 3 and 50 rue du Cherche-Midi, 6e, which is also a beauty salon, offers 20% off. Two reliable family-run discount businesses are **Catherine,** 6 rue de Castiglione, 1er, and **Maréchal,** 232 rue de Rivoli, 1er. If what you know you want happens to be a **Guerlain,** you must head for one of their own exclusive boutiques, at 2 pl. Vendôme, 1er; 29 rue de Sèvres, 6e; 68 av. des Champs-Elysées, 8e; or 93 rue de Passy, 16e.

If your main aim is to sniff a wide variety of perfumes, aim either for the **Galeries Lafayette** or **Au Printemps** near the Opéra, or **Sephora,** 50 rue de Passy, 16e, and the Forum des Halles. Sephora claims to be the world's largest perfumery store.

FASHION

If you can afford **haute couture**—and make no mistake, we're talking big bucks—sally forth to the av. Montaigne, 8e. Here you'll find such hardy perennials as **Christian Dior, Guy Laroche, Nina Ricci,** and **Emanuel Ungaro.** Alternatively, make your way to the rue du Faubourg St.-Honoré, 8e, for **Hermès, Lanvin,** and **Christian Lacroix.** Most of the other big names are in streets adjoining one of these two: **Balmain, Courrèges** and **Ted Lapidus** in the rue François-1er; **Givenchy** and **Yves Saint-Laurent** in the av. George-V; **Chloé** in the av. Franklin-Roosevelt; **Chanel** in the rue Cambon.

St.-Germain-des-Prés is the place for more avant-garde styles. Try any of the following *couture* designers: **Sonia Rykiel,** 4 rue de Grenelle, plus **Laura Ashley** (#34 and 94 rue de Rennes), **Kenzo** (on the corner of bvd. Raspail), and **Claude Montana** (#31); and **Chantal Thomass,** 11 rue Madame, and many long-famous boutiques such as **Dorothée Bis,** 33 rue de Sèvres; **Anastasia,** 18 rue de l'Ancienne-Comédie; **Gudule,** 72 rue St.-André-des-Arts, and **Tiffany,** 12 rue de Sèvres. All of these specialize in ready-to-wear. You'll also find a wealth of attractive and up-to-the-minute fashions in the huge number of boutiques in and around the bvd. St.-Germain. **La Gaminerie,** 137 bvd. St.-Germain, is an old favorite, with good accessories too.

The place des Victoires, near the newly renovated Les Halles district, has become one of *the* centers of avant-garde fashion. Come here for **Victoires, Thierry Mugler, Cacherel,** and **Corinne Sarrut.** The rue du Jour, leading off from Les Halles, is a favorite with lovers of sophisticated yet wearable outfits, while **Marithé et François Girbaud** on nearby rue Etienne Marcel is also very popular.

ACCESSORIES

The rue Tronchet is a good place for accessories. **La Bagagerie** at #12 is a reliable store for beautiful bags and purses to go with your new outfit, while **Carel** at #4 has really fabulous shoes, as does **Renast** at #33. **Hélion,** at #22, specializes in sleek gloves. The city's most famous sellers of leather goods are all in this part of Paris, with the great **Hermès** a short walk away in the fbg. St.-Honoré, at #24, and two major specialists at #265 and #271 rue St.-Honoré: **La Cour** and **Sellerie de France. Lancel,** in the place de l'Opéra, is another good bet.

On the Left Bank are several good shoe shops: **Carel** in the rue du Four, and at 78 rue des St.-Pères, **Cassandre, Céline,** and **Charles Jourdan** in the rue de Rennes, **François Villon** at 58 rue Bonaparte, and trendy **Maud Frizon** at 79 rue des St.-Pères.

Most of the city's fashion boutiques sell some accessories carefully selected to go with their outfits, and you should also consider examining the huge range of bags and purses, silk headscarves, and fashionable umbrellas in the department stores. Some of the open-air markets have bargains in shoes and bags, too. And talking of bargains, you may like to know about the **Club des 10,** 58 rue du fbg. St.-Honoré, 8e, which offers 30–40% off designs by some of the best-known *couture* and ready-to-wear names.

EDIBLE GOODIES

Pretty boxes of French regional specialties can be found in many places in Paris, from the little corner grocery or bakery to the gastronomic temples, such as those two *very* superior grocers, **Fauchon,** at 26 pl. de la Madeleine, 8e, or **Hédiard,** also in the pl. de la Madeleine, at #21, and at 126 rue du Bac, 7e, 106 bvd. de Courcelles, 17e, and in the Forum des Halles.

Those with a sweet tooth will be tempted by the *fruits confits* (candied fruit) of southern France, or by local specialties such as *calissons d'Aix* or *bergamotes de Nancy,* as well as many other types of sweets or candies. Delicious nougat from Montélimar comes in all shapes, sizes, and colors. Beautifully arranged boxes of wrapped hard candy are a delight to the eye as well as the palate, while perhaps nicest of all, and very typically French, are the delightful yet inexpensive little boxes or oval tins of *réglisse* (licorice), whose presentation hasn't changed for centuries. **A la Mère de Famille,** 1 rue de Provence, 9e, and 35 rue du Fbg. Montmartre, 9e, and **Jadis et Gourmande,** 88 bvd. Port Royal, 5e, and 27 rue Boissy d'Anglas, 8e, both have excellent selections of traditional French candies.

For great French chocolates try **Ballotin**, 43 rue Montorgueil, 2e, close to Les Halles.

Tins or cans of *foie gras,* or truffles, will delight a gourmet's heart. Snails and preserved wild mushrooms in cans or glass jars are other delicacies you won't find easily back home.

As for wine, corner groceries or the **Nicolas** chain of wine shops will suit your picnic needs, and will provide bottles to take home if you prefer not to use the duty-free shops at the airports. But if you want something really special, don't miss **Vins Rares et de Collection**, 25 rue Royale, 8e, which has a large selection of France's most famous vintages.

If you do plan to take home any food products, remember that you may not import into the US any fresh meats, fruits, plants, or other agricultural products.

GORGEOUS GIFTS

For those who want to find a more unusual gift we've picked out a few places that have something really special on offer.

For instance, **Isabelle Valogne**, 53 av. de la Bourdonnais, 7e, specializes in charming scent bottles, both antique and modern, and also has some fine Art Deco brooches. **La Rose des Vents**, 77 rue St.-Louis en l'Ile, 4e, is a pretty little shop with a good range of "natural products"—pots pourris, scented soaps, dried flowers, natural beauty products, candles, and the like. **Monsieur Renard**, 6 rue de l'Echaudé, 6e, is full of antique dolls and automata. **Le Monde en Marche**, 34 rue Dauphine, 6e, with many wooden toys and puppets, is a good place for presents for small children. **Françoise Thibault**, 1 rue Bourbon-le-Château, 6e, is an old favorite for attractive gifts, with some delightful handpainted boxes and picture frames. **Léon**, 220 rue de Rivoli, 1er, has been going for over 100 years, and is a must for magical little porcelain boxes decorated with flowers, exquisite thimbles, and paperweights, as well as reproductions of Sèvres porcelain.

If you prefer to take home an antique object, try the **Louvre des Antiquaires** emporium in the pl. du Palais-Royal, 1er, the **Village Suisse**, 78 av. de Suffren, 15e, or the **Cour des Saints-Pères**, 54 av. de la Motte Piquet, 15e. **Carré Rive Gauche** is the prime hunting ground for antiques on the Left Bank. A number of small dealers are grouped along the narrow streets of rue du Bac, rue de Beaune, rue de Lille, rue de l'Université, rue des Sts.-Pères, rue Jacob, and quai Voltaire.

And for art-lovers a print makes a good buy. The best area to try is the rue de Seine, 6e, and the surrounding streets, including the bookstalls along by the river. On the Right Bank, the happiest hunting ground is the avenue Matignon, 8e, but prices here are high. The **Département Chalcographique** in the Louvre, containing thousands of prints from old plates, is another must if you've set your heart on a print.

INDEX

Index

Notes

Notes

Fodor's Travel Guides

U.S. Guides

Alaska
Arizona
Atlantic City & the
  New Jersey Shore
Boston
California
Cape Cod
Carolinas & the
  Georgia Coast
The Chesapeake Region
Chicago
Colorado
Disney World & the
  Orlando Area

Florida
Hawaii
Las Vegas
Los Angeles, Orange
  County, Palm Springs
Maui
Miami,
  Fort Lauderdale,
  Palm Beach
Michigan, Wisconsin,
  Minnesota
New England
New Mexico
New Orleans

New Orleans (Pocket
  Guide)
New York City
New York City (Pocket
  Guide)
New York State
Pacific North Coast
Philadelphia
The Rockies
San Diego
San Francisco
San Francisco (Pocket
  Guide)
The South

Texas
USA
Virgin Islands
Virginia
Waikiki
Washington, DC

Foreign Guides

Acapulco
Amsterdam
Australia, New Zealand,
  The South Pacific
Austria
Bahamas
Bahamas (Pocket
  Guide)
Baja & the Pacific
  Coast Resorts
Barbados
Beijing, Guangzhou &
  Shanghai
Belgium &
  Luxembourg
Bermuda
Brazil
Britain (Great Travel
  Values)
Budget Europe
Canada
Canada (Great Travel
  Values)
Canada's Atlantic
  Provinces
Cancun, Cozumel,
  Yucatan Peninsula

Caribbean
Caribbean (Great
  Travel Values)
Central America
Eastern Europe
Egypt
Europe
Europe's Great
  Cities
France
France (Great Travel
  Values)
Germany
Germany (Great Travel
  Values)
Great Britain
Greece
The Himalayan
  Countries
Holland
Hong Kong
Hungary
India,
  including Nepal
Ireland
Israel
Italy

Italy (Great Travel
  Values)
Jamaica
Japan
Japan (Great Travel
  Values)
Kenya, Tanzania,
  the Seychelles
Korea
Lisbon
Loire Valley
London
London (Great
  Travel Values)
London (Pocket Guide)
Madrid & Barcelona
Mexico
Mexico City
Montreal &
  Quebec City
Munich
New Zealand
North Africa
Paris
Paris (Pocket Guide)
People's Republic of
  China

Portugal
Rio de Janeiro
The Riviera (Fun on)
Rome
Saint Martin &
  Sint Maarten
Scandinavia
Scandinavian Cities
Scotland
Singapore
South America
South Pacific
Southeast Asia
Soviet Union
Spain
Spain (Great Travel
  Values)
Sweden
Switzerland
Sydney
Tokyo
Toronto
Turkey
Vienna
Yugoslavia

Special-Interest Guides

Health & Fitness
  Vacations
Royalty Watching

Selected Hotels of
  Europe

Selected Resorts and
  Hotels of the U.S.
Shopping in Europe

Skiing in North America
Sunday in New York